THE
~wholesome
junk food~
COOKBOOK

THE

wholesome
junk food

COOKBOOK

MORE THAN 100 *Healthy Recipes*
FOR EVERYDAY SNACKING

by Laura Trice

RUNNING PRESS
PHILADELPHIA · LONDON

Library of Congress Control Number: 2009941884

ISBN 978-0-7624-3801-3

Edited by Geoffrey Stone
Cover and interior design by Amanda Richmond
Typography: ITC Avant Garde, Lomba, and Rockwell
Food styling by Maria Person

The publishers would like to express their gratitude to the following providers for their
invaluable assistance in the production of this book Manor Home, Philadelphia, PA;
Open House, Philadelphia, PA; Scarlett Alley, Philadelphia, PA; Crate & Barrel, King of Prussia, PA

Running Press Book Publishers
2300 Chestnut Street
Philadelphia, PA 19103-4371

Visit us on the web!
www.runningpresscooks.com

table *of* contents

Acknowledgments

First, to my mother, Sally Breyer Trice, who had me cooking from the moment I showed interest at age two. She allowed my sisters, Stefanie and Elizabeth—and all the kids in the neighborhood—and me to cook and bake without ever admonishing us for dropping eggs on the floor or breaking a dish. The kitchen was a free space for creativity and experimentation. I created my first original recipe of cottage cheese and raisins in a lettuce cup at age three. My mom wrote it down on a recipe card and still has it. Thank you, Mom, for teaching me about healthy eating, giving me both a healthy body and the knowledge of how to make great-tasting food that is also good for me. I also appreciate all of Mom's help in testing the many recipes in this book, and for sharing the photo she took of me baking that is on every Laura's Wholesome Junk Food cookie tub.

Thank you to my grandmother, Helen Breyer, who is no longer with us, for teaching my mother to cook. Grandma moved from the hustle and bustle of Manhattan to a small country farm and had six children that she had to stretch every penny to feed. Everything was homemade and as healthy as she could make it. I am in her kitchen, baking cookies, on the Laura's Wholesome Junk Food label photo.

Thank you to my friends, Cole, Lisa, Heidi, Katelyn, and Pat's girls. Thank you to my sisters, Stefanie and Elizabeth, and brother-in-law, Mark. To Erika Penzer Kerekes, an amazing woman, writer (in Erika's kitchen), and chef, who contributed recipes that I enjoyed eating many times, and also took me in during a difficult period. To Karen, Char, Sharon, Perry, Joe, and Rich, all people who believe in me and make Laura's Wholesome Junk Food and Dr. Laura tick! And a very special thank you to my teachers and advisors, Geoffrey, Dr. Pat, Laurel, Ira, Patricia, Carole, and David.

To Char and my mom, thank you for the editing help. You ladies made all the difference in the world with your insights and suggestions. (Mom, a former English teacher, reread this many times during a very busy time to make sure it was just right.)

I appreciate my agent, Andrea Hurst,

who took a chance on a first time author, and Jonathan Kirsch, Esq., who helped with the details. Thank you, Running Press for your expertise. To Geoffrey Stone, my patient editor, who guided this to be better than I imagined, and Amanda Richmond, Frances Soo Ping Chow, and Steve Legato, whose visual gifts made it delicious to look at. Thank you to my generous contributors, Mom, Cole, Erika, Mrs. Arciero, and Linda Stone, who shared a select few of their secret recipes with me.

Sally Breyer Trice

Introduction

· ·

Let's face it: everybody likes junk food. We have become accustomed to eating foods with high levels of refined sugars, processed grains, and ingredients that require a PhD in organic chemistry to pronounce. Why has this become so common among prepared foods? Essentially, companies have replaced nature's own ingredients with highly processed products and chemicals to reduce costs, extend shelf life, and raise profits. Excessive salt, sugar, and preservatives are added to replace taste that is lost when using lower-quality ingredients. And the term *natural* is misleading and does not necessarily mean wholesome or healthy anymore.

As a child, I looked longingly at the popular and trendy packaged goods others were eating. I was the one with the bag lunches packed with homemade cookies, carrot sticks, whole-grain bread, and fruit. I was upset. I felt that if my mom really cared, I'd have chips and candy like the other kids. Every chance I got, I went to friends' homes to eat their junk food. Later, in college, I found myself a little heavy and low on energy, and I wasn't sure why. The "why" was

because I was no longer eating my mom's wholesome food on a daily basis.

I got into healthy eating because I am what is called a *foodie*. I love the taste, texture, and enjoyment of good food. However, I noticed that my pants got tight when I ate certain things, and I did not like that. I also noticed that other foods made me feel tired. In medical school, I realized that a lot of the sick patients had eating habits that were just like mine, and their illnesses were caused or irritated by poor food choices over long periods of time. We often liked to eat what tasted good, without considering ingredient quality and the long-term impact of our choices.

That is when the concept of Laura's Wholesome Junk Food was born. I set out to prove that with careful planning and wholesome ingredients, you could make cookies that taste great *and* are nutritious, with full ingredient disclosure and transparency. It was not easy. In fact, I remade each Bite-lette recipe twenty to forty times to get it just right.

I eventually came upon the right healthy recipe to make an amazing little cookie whose only difference was the use of higher-quality, wholesome ingredients. For example, I used dates instead of white sugar or high-fructose corn syrup, and expeller-pressed oil instead of hydrogenated or chemically extracted oil.

I constantly receive e-mails from happy customers who tell me how much they love the cookies or that they are the only healthy cookies their kids or husband will eat. All over the United States, people have our Bite-lettes in their pantries, desk drawers, lunch boxes, cars, and fridges.

The concept I applied to the first Laura's Wholesome Junk Food cookie recipe is not unique to cookies. My mom's recipes used applesauce instead of granulated sugar for cakes. She sweetened muffins with honey and bananas. You will find that I do the same.

While I was writing this cookbook, a friend wrote, "Since you are working on a wholesome junk food cookbook, do you have a healthy recipe for whoopie pies?" That is my kind of project. Yes, we do! It is in the cake section.

I started Laura's Wholesome Junk Food as a way to share the healthy, great-tasting cookies I had created for myself and others. Now, I've created this book to share my knowledge, expertise, and recipes with you. For years, customers have been requesting a cookbook that had tasty foods that were also wholesome. So, here are my recipes as a way to share with all of you the favorite treats I grew up with and a few I discovered as an adult. I hope you enjoy these simple, delicious, and homemade foods.

I want this book to be more than just a cookbook for you. I want you to feel more confident, empowered, and at peace about what you are eating. The best thank-you will be the knowledge that you are enjoying your food and feeling great about you and your family's health. Never mind the low-fat, low-carbohydrate trend; come on in to Laura's Wholesome Junk Food's kitchen for your favorite desserts and snacks.

In joy and good health,
Dr. Laura

Part 1: HEALTHY EATING

CHAPTER 1

Better Diet

I love food! I love sweets!

I love junk food!

Food is about joy and sharing meals with those we love. Food is fun to create and fun to eat. It is a pleasure to nourish the bodies we have been given. American traditions revolve around food, especially "junk" food. There's the ice cream social, the bake sale, Cracker Jacks, and apple pie. The American diet used to consist of high-fat comfort foods, but we also did more physical activity, and the food had better, less-processed ingredients.

We seem to be coming full circle, with the best from the past and also new improvements. In the previous century we learned how to refine sugar, flour, and fat and create inexpensive foods that have long shelf lives and look pretty—only to realize that the ingredients we used before doing all that processing were actually better for us. We are truly in a discovery process when it comes to food and how to best care for our bodies while also pleasing our taste buds.

Today, scientists and the government look at health and food and make recommendations to make our food better for us through, for example, enrichment (adding back what was taken out in processing—like enriching flour with B vitamins) and fortification (adding something that was never there, like calcium to orange juice). But it is really our job as individuals to stay aware, use our good sense, and practice consistent body care, inside and out, to the best of our ability. No one has every food answer; one minute we are told something is good for us, and the next we are told it is not. My goal here is to combine current information, my personal experience, and what makes sense to me in an easy-to-understand and fun-to-read book.

Many cookbooks talk about better foods. I am focusing on better sweets and snacks, as I feel that that is where most of us get in trouble. We say we will allow ourselves another "treat," or we snack so frequently on unhealthy snacks that we are negatively impacted by high amounts of refined salt, sugar, and trans fats.

Traditional American favorites have gotten a lot of bad press lately, and I disagree with what is being said. It's not the food choices that are the problem; it is just a few of the ingredients. Am I really supposed to give up the foods that are fun for me and my family to make and eat? Are we really supposed to consume bran instead? I don't think so. These foods are part of our heritage and traditions. I love the foods we all enjoy eating for desserts and snacks, and I think they taste *great*. I, for one, do not want to give them up! Nor do we need to. We either need to get these recipes back to the wholesomeness they once had, or use one or two new, high-quality ingredients that are better for us but were not readily available when our grandmothers came up with the recipes. Today there is a new awareness about food sensitivities to things such as milk, eggs, and certain grains that many of us have to work around. This cookbook also takes that into consideration.

Crib Notes for Decoding Food Labels

One main way to have a better diet is to understand more about your body and what it needs. Our bodies need certain types of food—yes, even fats—to thrive. However, we do not need all the unpronounceable ingredients that have been added to increase shelf life and decrease cost. Our bodies were created to break down and process foods, and our bodies do not like everything to be preprocessed before being eaten. Yet so many foods have processed salts, refined sugars, artificial colors and flavors, and preservatives. And they often contain hydrogenated oils that contain trans fats as well as animal products from unhealthily raised animals who receive hormones to make them grow faster and antibiotics to cure illness caused by cramped living conditions. When I read most ingredient labels, I find words that are difficult to pronounce, even with my degrees in chemistry and medicine.

For a long time I have been wondering why so many people are eating foods that make them gain weight, feel tired, or develop other health problems. I have come to understand that there is a direct correlation between what people eat and how they feel. I want you to understand what a better diet is and to help you decode the food labels so you know what to look for.

The quick foodie rundown is that all food is made up of three basic things: carbohydrates (like baked potato or fruits), protein (like eggs or fish), and fats (like olive oil or butter). So, what are all those other things that I can't pronounce? Most often they are artificial ingredients, chemicals, or "gobbledygook," as my mom called them when I was growing up.

This section may look intimidating; however, if you are willing to get through it, you will understand food much better. If you still have questions, please visit my Web site at *www.lauraswholesomejunkfood.com* or e-mail me at *Dr laura@lwjf.net*.

How do I eat? I allow myself to nibble on raw nuts, fruits, and vegetables throughout the day, without worrying about quantity. I do watch the quality and amount of treats, animal products, and starches that I eat. My particular guideline is that I do not bring white flour or white sugar into my house. I know myself! If there is something in the house that is not good for me—let's say a cake or chips—I will eat more than I want to in an evening and then not feel good the next day. That is me. You may have more discipline that that.

If you look at mainstream news, you will hear the suggestion that people eat low-fat, low-carbohydrate diets; that leaves primarily protein. I vote for a balanced mix of the three, using high-quality ingredients. We will take a look at each of these.

Fat

Let's start by tackling the one with the most misinformation circulating: *fats*. Contrary to popular opinion, fat is not a bad thing. Fat is your friend. In fact, fat helps us feel satisfied and provides us with important nutrients that our bodies need. For example, fats are an essential part of maintaining healthy skin and hair. They protect the body's organs, help the body keep its right temperature, and support cell function. Furthermore, fats act as energy stores and actually help defend the body against diseases.

We have all heard about essential fatty acids and how important the omega fats are. We can understand all fats best by understanding where they come from and how they look at room temperature.

TWO SOURCES OF FAT

Where do fats come from? Fat can come from animal or vegetable sources. Butter and fish oil are examples of animal fats. Plant fats include flaxseed oil and olive oil. (Oils are in the fat family, so I will use *oil* and *fat* interchangeably, even though we tend to think of fat as solid and oil as a liquid. However, you will only see "fat" on food labels, because all oils are fats.) But are all fats equal?

SATURATED VERSUS UNSATURATED

What does the fat look like at room temperature? This is very important in understanding fats. They are either naturally solid at room temperature (like butter) or liquid (like olive oil). If a fat is solid at room temperature, it is called *saturated* because it naturally has more hydrogen in it; if it is liquid at room temperature, it is called *unsaturated* because it naturally has less hydrogen, making it easier for the body to break it down. So, coconut oil is a naturally saturated vegetable oil (solid at room temp), and olive oil is a naturally unsaturated vegetable oil (liquid at room temp). Butter is a naturally saturated animal fat (solid at room temp), and fish oil is a naturally unsaturated animal fat (liquid at room temp).

BAD FATS

The fats that are not your friend are called *trans fats*, and they do not occur naturally; they are man-made. Trans fats are very hard for the body to break down, as they are artificially saturated (solid at room temperature) and were created only to make food last longer and cost less. They are not designed with your health in mind. I will tell you how to spot them so you can avoid them. There are also new regulations that require companies to put the amount of "trans fats" in the white nutritional label on every food item. Ideally, you should only buy products that say "0 trans fats."

So what are trans fats, and where do they come from? Sometimes, companies pump hydrogen into a liquid vegetable oil to extend its shelf life. That creates a solid fat that contains trans fats. Avoid trans fats or anything that has "hydrogenated" or "partially hydrogenated" fats in the ingredient listing. Instead, use extra-virgin olive oil, organic butter, coconut oil, or an expeller-pressed oil for your eating, cooking, and baking. You'll get the great taste and feeling of satisfaction that fat provides, while your body gets what it needs without being harmed.

WHAT I BUY

I buy expeller-pressed oils, organic oils, and extra-virgin olive oil. Other oils tend to be "solvent extracted," which means that a chemical was used to extract the oil. I prefer oils that have been squeezed out naturally. For animal fats, I like butter. I suggest that if you are going to spend any extra money on buying organic, spend it on organic animal products, like organic butter, because they will be free of the hormones and antibiotics routinely fed to animals that are conventionally raised.

Carbohydrates

Carbohydrates have gotten a bad reputation, but I have good news for you. Carbs are good for you; you need them to live. They have a very important function: they feed your brain. You just need to eat unrefined carbohydrates as much as possible, and watch portion size. When you think carbohydrates, think comfort food: pasta, corn bread, fruit, sweets, rice, and bagels. But which are good, and which are bad?

Processed carbohydrates include anything that does not get picked from a plant or come from the ground. For example, an apple or sweet potato is picked and you eat it. It is not processed by anything but your mouth and body. But a cupcake does not grow on anything and has been made from wheat and sugarcane, processed into white flour and sugar. These are the carbs that we need to minimize. In the processing, they are stripped of their naturally occurring trace minerals and fiber. I believe that is why they make me feel tired or bloated, where an unrefined carb, like a peach, does not. It is hard to avoid processed foods; however, it is critical to emphasize the unprocessed ones in your diet.

Protein

Most of us know that pro- tein builds muscle, but it is also needed by other parts of the body. Just like fats, proteins are divided into the same two categories of animal and plant sources. Examples of animal protein are beef, fish, and eggs. Vegetable proteins include tofu, lentils, and dried beans, such as the pinto.

When considering animal proteins, I suggest that you buy organic eggs, meats, and animal products to keep antibiotics and hormones out of your system. Free-range isn't necessarily organic, but it is also a good choice. *Free-range* means that there are usually (read the label) no hormones or antibiotics added to the products and that the animals from which these foods come have a certain amount of space in which to wander around. (This is thought to be more humane and to produce a higher quality product.) I buy free-range products that clearly state "no hormones or antibiotics added" when available simply because they are high quality and often less expensive than organic.

Our Food

Most foods are a mixture of fats, protein, and carbohydrates. Our mini English muffin pizzas, for example, have fat, carbohydrates, and protein. The pepperoni contains fat and some protein. The cheese has fat, protein, and some carbohydrates, and the crust is made of unrefined spelt flour, which is a partially refined carbohydrate. But beyond a food's ingredient, does it matter where our food comes from? Let's consider two available sources of food for purchase.

Retail Foods vs Food Service Foods

Retail means you pick it off the shelf yourself and buy it in a store, usually wrapped. Food service means it was unpackaged, sitting behind a glass counter, as in a coffee shop, or served to you in a restaurant or at a deli counter. It is called "food service" because someone else had to hand it to you.

FOOD SERVICE

How does food being packaged or not packaged impact your health? When the food is not packaged, you have less access to the nutritional information. The FDA (Food and Drug Administration) requires retail products to list the ingredients and nutritional facts on the package, but food service does not provide this information on the product. There is no place to list a donut's nutritional facts, because the donut is unwrapped. Because of this, all coffee shops and delis should have calorie and nutritional information available on request to you, but often they "can't find the binder," or you can't locate the nutritional information on their Web site. One popular chain that offers many 500- to 600-calorie muffins and scones has had the nutritional section of their Web site "under construction" for over a year now. The only thing you can find is the list of snacks and drinks under 200 calories. Apparently they have not had time to list the food value of the many other higher-calorie items. I had to call for a week, spending several hours of my time, to learn that the most popular muffin contained almost 700 calories. My feeling is that they may not want you to know that you are consuming 1,000 calories with a hot drink and muffin. Of course, you may pick their 450-calorie "Reduced-fat" muffin. But did you realize that they can call anything "reduced-fat" if they originally made a worse version? If you have a favorite latte and muffin, my suggestion is to pester the coffee shop until they tell you how many calories you are eating and how many servings that muffin represents. It may be 3 servings, so you may want to break it into thirds and save the rest for a friend or another day.

Know what you are eating! Some states are now requiring by law that coffee shops and restaurants post the calorie counts. But even if they don't, when you are at a restaurant and your common sense tells you that the food is rich or the portion is huge, you have a decision to make. You can choose to split a salad and entrée with someone, so you both will eat less. Sometimes I just split two to three appetizers with someone for my meal. If you are intent upon cleaning your plate, you will often eat more than your body needs. Try eating only half of your meal, and take a doggie bag home for later. Cleaning your plate when the food is rich or the portion is large is not a good strategy. Sometimes, too, we tend to eat too much when we are in a rush. Slow down. It takes some time for your body to tell your brain that you are full; this is why eating slowly helps you eat less.

RETAIL

As I mentioned, retail product packaging must provide nutritional information on the label—but it can be a little tricky to read. The nutrition facts can be found on cereal boxes, chip bags, etc., and are usually printed in a box or typed out on a line, if the package is small.

Here is an example of what you'll see when you look for a product's nutrition information. These just happen to be the nutrition facts for Laura's Wholesome Junk Food's best-selling cookie:

our Oatmeal Chocolate Chip Bite-lette. Don't be intimidated by this label. It is important that you glance at just a few key things here, and I'll walk you through it.

Oatmeal Chocolate Chip Bite-lettes

NUTRITION FACTS: Serv size: 2 Bite-lettes (~25g), Servings per pkg. 7, Per Serving: Calories 110, Fat Cal. 50, Total Fat 5g (7% DV), Sat. Fat 1.5g (7% DV), Trans Fat 0g, Cholest 0mg (0% DV), Sodium 88mg (4% DV), Potassium 53mg (2% DV), Total Carb. 14g (4% DV), Dietary Fiber 1.2g (5% DV), Sugars 7.5g, Protein 2g, Vitamin A (0% DV), Vitamin C (0% DV), Calcium (1% DV), Iron (3% DV). Percent Daily Values are based on a 2,000 calorie diet.

Let's start with serving size and calories. In this case, ours is 2 Bite-lettes at 110 calories for 2. So, that would be about 55 calories for each cookie. All the remaining numbers relate to your eating the serving size of 2 cookies.

Serving size and calories are the first things I look at. Why? Let's say you buy a packaged cookie or muffin and glance quickly at the nutrition facts section. It says 150 calories, so you eat your treat, feeling good about your choice. But often if you look at serving size, it might say "3 servings per package." Do you realize that all of the numbers on that label—fat, sugar, and salt content—are based on that muffin or cookie being broken up into 3 pieces, and that *each piece* has 150 calories? If you ate the entire muffin or cookie yourself, which most of us do, that means you ate 3 servings and therefore had 450 calories, not 150. One serving of grains is about the size of a cassette tape. That is approximately the thickness of your pinkie and the width of two business cards side by side. So you can see that a regular bagel could easily be 2 to 4 grain servings, and you may be counting it as one.

The next category is fat. As you can see from the label above, one serving of Bite-lettes contains 5 grams. Types of fat include saturated, unsaturated, and trans fats. The trans fats are the most important to look at. You want to see 0, as you do here. Food suppliers must tell you the amount of trans fats, since they are harmful.

Carbohydrates are next on the label, and these, like fats, start with the total amount. Total carbohydrates for the 2 cookies are 14 grams. Of those 14 grams, 1.2 grams are dietary fiber, which we know is important for good

health, and 7.5 grams would be categorized as sugar. (We use high-quality, natural sugar sources in our cookies.)

So, what are those "% DV" numbers, and what do they mean? DV stands for Daily Value. In this case the dietary fiber is listed as 5% DV. The FDA-recommended diet on which these nutritional facts are based is a 2,000-calorie diet for an average person. (People who are more active or have higher metabolism may need more.) The government also recommends certain amounts of fat, cholesterol, carbohydrates, sodium, and many other substances, with the idea that you need those quantities and to go over them would not be healthy. So, when we see that the 2 Bite-lettes provide 5% DV for dietary fiber, it means that you get 5% of the daily value of fiber recommended for each day. You need 24 more grams of fiber to reach 100% DV.

To simplify this, what the nutrition facts really say is, "Here is how much we suggest you eat of this product, and if you follow our advice, this is the nutritional value you will receive. We are also warning you about things like salt, cholesterol, and trans fats that should be limited."

Next on our label is the listing of ingredients for the Oatmeal Chocolate Chip Bite-lettes. You will find similar labels on all packaged foods.

Oatmeal Chocolate Chip Bite-lettes

INGREDIENTS: Rolled oats, chocolate chips (dehydrated cane juice, unsweetened chocolate, cocoa butter, soy lecithin, pure vanilla), date paste, 100% expeller-pressed canola oil, evaporated cane juice, fruit juice, natural grain dextrins, unbleached enriched wheat flour, unsweetened coconut, water, non-GMO soy protein isolate, non-GMO soy powder, baking powder (non-aluminum), sea salt, orange oil and citric acid.

Ingredients must be listed by quantity, determined by weight, with the ingredient used most listed first, and the ingredient used the least listed last. As you can see, we use more rolled oats than any other ingredient, as compared to a tiny amount of sea salt. When you see something in parentheses, these are the ingredients found in the immediately preceding item. For example, the ingredients used in our chocolate chips are those listed in parentheses following the words *chocolate chips* (dehydrated cane juice, unsweetened chocolate, etc.).

Date paste is our primary sweetener. It comes from dates that are picked from a tree and is used in its natural, unprocessed state. Date paste is dates that have had the pits removed and are mashed.

Evaporated cane juice is a whole sugar with its trace minerals and nutrients still present. Fruit juice is just that: juice from fruits. *Natural grain dextrins* is a fancy term for rice syrup. Why did we use a fancy term? This is the official name for the type of rice syrup we use. Unbleached enriched flour is regular wheat flour that has the bran and germ removed but has not been bleached or bromated (another health-compromising chemical process to increase the volume of baked goods; if the label says simply "wheat flour," you can bet that flour has been bleached and bromated). Our coconut is ordered specially without the preservative sodium bisulfate, which is used as a whitening and anti-caking agent. The word *non-GMO* (not genetically modified) tells you that we paid more for higher quality, more natural soy products that have not been genetically tampered with. Many baking powders contain aluminum, deemed undesirable for us. We use baking powder that does not have it.

Orange oil and citric acid are the oil from an orange skin and citric acid that comes from fruit, such as lemons and oranges. You may ask, "Why did you not use orange peel for the orange flavor? That would seem more natural." Well, I started off using fresh orange peel, which is made up of many components, including fiber, orange oil, and citric acid. But for some reason, the fiber got a bitter taste when baked, so we began using the oil and citric acid to give our cookies the orange tang.

One trick found on some labels is disguising sugar with different names. Don't be fooled. A label that lists dextrose, sucrose, glucose, and maltodextrin has just named four types of processed sugar in one product.

Eat 'Em Up

You have every right to eat your favorite sweets and comfort foods, and by becoming more aware of portion size and ingredient choices, you will feel good eating those foods again. By "favorite," I mean the treats or snacks you go back to over and over again.

There are five keys to a better diet that make the difference between eating your favorite foods and being healthy, and not being healthy: *quality*, *quantity*, *quickness*, *activity*, and *rest*. You may wonder how activity and rest are parts of a healthy diet. I'm using *diet* here in a broader sense that encompasses all areas of our lives that contribute to our well-being. Activity stretches our bodies and burns off the calories we consume, and rest is what we need to rejuvenate for another day. We will go over these one by one.

Quality refers to the superiority of one ingredient over another, for instance, substituting fruit as a sweetener in place of white sugar. We will discuss ingredient quality and how you can choose better ingredients in the next chapter.

Quantity means how much food you consume. We really can make and enjoy the foods we have loved our entire lives; we just need to eat less of them. Bigger or more is not better. Tricky or hidden labeling can often lead to your eating more than you meant to. By learning to make your favorites foods in this book, you will be able to enjoy what you are eating without being tricked into consuming more than you should.

Quickness means how fast we eat our food. In today's fast-paced society, we often eat so quickly, versus "dining," that we end up consuming more than we should, because we don't give the body enough time to tell us, "I'm full." Again, slow down. By reading labels and baking for yourself, you will improve your awareness. So, even if you overeat once in a while due to rushing around, it is not that big a deal, because your ingredients are of higher quality, and you have more leeway. Still, take the time to enjoy your food and think through your choices.

Activity means that the more we move, the more food we can enjoy. Many of us forget to take the time or do not have the luxury of extra time daily to exercise and play. Honestly, if it isn't fun, I won't do it. I do not work out alone in a gym. I prefer to do exercise with others, and outdoors, when possible. I'm happy visiting with friends, so I structure my exercise to include them. You will often see me taking a walk or biking with friends. I also do little things that do not seem significant, but they add up. For instance, I park far away from the grocery store to walk to it. I take the stairs up a couple of flights, instead of the elevator, when given the choice. When I'm feeling low on energy, I try to get someone to go for a short walk with me, even if it is just ten minutes around the block. I stretch if I am bored waiting in line, and try to touch my toes.

Rest is another important aspect of staying healthy. As with activity, you need a balanced "diet" of rest to keep your body functioning properly. I need good sleep every night and do best when I get to bed by 9 or 10 p.m. How many of us stay up too late, don't feel well, and therefore not only make unhealthy food choices but also decide to not exercise the next day? For me, everything starts with sleep. And even though I am a healthy woman, I get a little tired every afternoon. (I think the siesta, a midday nap, exists for a reason.) When I feel that way, I go somewhere quiet, when possible, close my eyes, and completely zone out for twenty to thirty minutes. I can actually feel my body relax, settle down, and revive again. We all have to push ourselves from time to time. That is part of life, but let's try to make it the exception. Adequate activity and rest are the foundation to building a healthy life.

Summary

Quality: Choose good ingredients, staying away from bad ones, like refined salt, white sugar, and trans fats.

Quantity: Know the portion size, and use common sense. Protein should fill up one quarter of a small plate, with a sweet potato, brown rice, or other whole grain or complex carbohydrate filling up another quarter, and green, red, and/or yellow vegetables filling up the other half.

Quickness: Learn something from traditions about dining versus eating quickly. Taking the time to eat slowly will enable you to realize when you are full so that you do not overstuff yourself.

Activity: Do activity at a level that is safe for you every day and that brings you joy. It needs to feel good to you, not like a chore.

Rest: Get to bed at a decent time to allow for enough (seven to nine hours) sleep each night.

You have perhaps heard the saying "You are what you eat," and there is a lot of truth to that. Therefore, in the pages to come, we are going to show you how to create a better diet for a healthier—and happier—you.

∽ CHAPTER 2 ∾
Better Ingredients

· ·

When my mom was growing up in the 1940s, her mother would bake many loaves of whole-grain bread for her family every week. Kneading bread dough was just one of many jobs she had to do on the family farm. Then, while my mom was still in school, white, mass-produced bread appeared in the stores. She remembers feeling embarrassed about her dark, homemade, whole-grain bread, since white bread was by then considered fashionable and better. When I was growing up, hydrogenated shortening with trans fats, white flour, and sugar had become the new standard, inexpensive way to make food that lasted a long time on the shelf, without regard to whether it was good for our bodies.

Nowadays, we have much more information on what is and is not good for us. When I began looking into the ingredients in snack foods, I was appalled. There had to be a way to make great-tasting food that was also good for me. Then I remembered my mom's cookbooks, with her handwriting in them. She'd replace sugar with applesauce, or use maple syrup when it called for corn syrup. She'd sweeten muffins with honey and bananas. These basic premises became the core of Laura's Wholesome Junk Food.

My first goal was to create a cookie recipe using quality ingredients, work on it until it was perfect, and then enjoy it guilt-free. Laura's Wholesome Junk Food now has ten flavors. I made each recipe many times, adjusting little things to make sure I had it just right. Our products are free of eggs and milk; however, customers soon started to ask for wheat- and gluten-free products, too, so we created those as well.

Laura's Wholesome Junk Food tastes as good as any other junk food but is made from high-quality ingredients. We use unprocessed sea salt instead of conventional table salt; wholesome sweeteners, like dates, fruit, and whole evaporated cane juice instead of white sugar and corn syrup; and higher-quality fats and oils instead of hydrogenated and trans fats. These premium ingredients, also used in this cookbook, will give you the same or better taste and will be healthier for your body since they are less refined.

Society has again returned to the basic nutritional whole grains that my mom's generation had veered away from. We also have more knowledge about unhealthy ingredients, like trans fats, white sugar, and additives that should be avoided in general. Many healthful natural foods, such as agave and maple syrup, have become more widely available than in the past. The best news is that today, we have a better selection of quality ingredients to work with and choose from than ever before.

Let's discuss a few terms you will see in this cookbook.

Gluten-free: A diet of foods that are free of gluten. Some people are unable to digest the gluten found in certain grains. Wheat, barley, and spelt are a few grains that contain gluten. Corn, rice, potato, and tapioca flours do not contain gluten. A big problem facing people on gluten-free diets is that so many products add a little bit of regular wheat flour, which can make them sick. They have to become experts at reading labels to protect their health.

Vegan: A diet where people only eat foods derived from plants.

Vegetarian: A diet where people eat plant-derived food but often eat cheeses and unfertilized eggs as well.

Food sensitivities/ allergies: Many people have to avoid certain foods either because they upset their digestive systems, cause hives, or produce even more severe symptoms. Wheat, soy, eggs, milk, tree nuts (like almonds or coconut), ground nuts (like peanuts), and shellfish are just a few common allergens. There are even people sensitive to dates, oranges, and oats.

the Fantastic Fourteen

And now, for the unveiling of our Fantastic Fourteen. These are high-quality ingredients that you will see in the recipes in this cookbook. If you stock them in your fridge, and buy products that contain them rather than their higher-refined counterparts, you will notice a marked difference in how you feel. Combine this with eliminating corn syrup, white sugar, white flour, and trans fats from your pantry and kitchen entirely, and you will be in excellent shape.

Many of us have sweet cravings, so you will notice that I focus on sweets a lot. I need to get my sweet cravings met, but in a way that is good for me. So here are some ingredients that help me do exactly that!

Agave syrup: Agave syrup comes from a cactus and is made by reducing a liquid down to a clear syrup. Agave syrup comes in light and dark colors, and both are good. You can also buy it raw or organic. It is a great, natural sweetener.

Dates: Dates grow on trees, are very sweet, and blend in nicely as a sweetener. They can be added to any smoothie to produce a creamy sweetness. Dates are the number one sweetener in all of Laura's Wholesome Junk Food Bite-lettes.

Evaporated cane juice (sugar): Whole evaporated cane juice is a whole sugar from the sugarcane plant. (When I say "whole," it means that the important parts of the food have not been removed.) It contains all of the trace minerals and nutrients that are removed in the normal sugar-refining process that results in empty-calorie white sugar and nutrient-rich molasses. Though it is called cane *juice*, it is really a granulated sugar that looks like brown sugar but is better for you. This can be confusing, because "juice" sounds as if it were liquid, which is why I call it evaporated cane juice crystals in the book. However, what it means is that the actual juice taken from the sugarcane has been evaporated. (There is a trend these days to say "organic cane sugar," yet that is nothing more than plain, white, granulated sugar with fewer trace minerals and molasses-like color than the whole version that I prefer.) I want you to have choices. The whole sugar does range from pale tan to dark brown in color. If you want a light or yellow cake, you might want to choose the pale tan cane sugar. If you want nutrition over color and do not mind the cake appearing a little darker, use a dark brown evaporated cane sugar. When making darker desserts like chocolate cake or a strawberry sauce, you can use the darker granulated whole cane sugar and it does not change the appearance. The more white the sugar, the fewer nutrients and less healthy it is for you. See the photos of Boston Cream Pie, Lemon Pound Cake, and Apple Pie. They all used darker sugars and whole grain flours. Our gluten-free apple pie used a white rice flour so you can see the difference between a light and dark flour and sweetener. They both taste delicious.

Fruit: There are lots of common fruits, like bananas, that you will see us using as sweeteners. These are, without exception, better for you than refined sugar.

Honey: Honey comes from honeybees and is a great sweetener. It comes in many different flavors, depending on what the bees are exposed to. Honey can come raw or pasteurized. I prefer raw, yet raw is not recommended for infants or others with weakened immune systems. Honey is supersweet, so in certain recipes it works, and in others it does not. Sometimes I use honey and another wholesome sweetener together: the honey to sweeten the recipe most of the way, and the other, less-intense sweetener to fine-tune it. Because honey comes from bees, it is considered an animal product by vegans, who will not eat it.

Maple syrup: Maple syrup comes from the sap of a maple tree and is boiled down to make a syrup. It was used traditionally on pancakes before less-expensive imitation maple syrup containing high-fructose corn syrup came along. Maple syrup is wonderful as a sweetener.

Molasses: Molasses is chock-full of nutrients and vitamins that add richness to this sweetener. It contains all the goodness that is removed from the sugarcane to make white sugar.

Here are the other seven main ingredients that are essential parts of our nutritious goodies:

Baking powder (nonaluminum): Non-aluminum baking powder is what it says—free of aluminum, which is often found in most baking powders. Scientists are still uncertain about the dangers of aluminum, but for me it's better to be safe.

Expeller-pressed or organic oils: These are oils that have not been chemically processed, so they are better for you. Other oils can be chemically extracted, but expeller and organic oils use pressure, not chemicals, to get the oil out. I prefer baking with oils and fats that feel natural to me. For sweet items I like to use a sunflower, safflower, or butter. Make sure that you buy expeller-pressed oils when possible. It means that chemical solvents have not been used in the processing. If all you can get is liquid vegetable oil, just make sure it has no trans fats. When possible, use organic butter. I like the salted version because I enjoy salt. I will often say just "oil" in the recipes, and I want you to use what you have on hand. Don't feel that you have to go out and get something new. Make sure your oil has not gone rancid. I use the sniff test. If it smells off (a little bitter), toss it because it has gone bad. I'll sometimes keep oils in the fridge so they last longer. Again, make sure that whatever you decided to use has zero trans fats. That is why I prefer the simplicity of a sunflower or safflower oil or butter. It is a straightforward and wholesome choice. For all the recipes in this book, use a good quality, expeller-pressed oil.

Milk and egg products: Organic, hormone-free, and/or antibiotic-free dairy and eggs are more wholesome than nonorganic because they do not have the additives found in factory-farmed products. Foods that come from animals that are on antibiotics or hormones could contain residues from those products, and these can interact with the human body. That is why I recommend spending the extra amount when possible on natural eggs and milk. Antibiotics and hormones are added only to cut costs and/or increase profits, not for our health or well-being. If you are allergic to dairy (milk and eggs), there are a number of good substitutes for milk (eggs will be difficult to replace). Try oat or soy, almond, or coconut milk. The flavor is slightly different, but it's still good. People following gluten-free diets should look for "gluten-free" alternative milk labels.

Salt: Unprocessed salt comes either from the ocean or is mined, and contains trace minerals. Unlike table salt, unprocessed salt has not been highly refined, so the color may not be pure white, and there may be little flecks in it. The crystals may also be bigger or irregularly shaped, and some sea salt seems almost sticky. Though I have not seen any scientific evidence for this, I find that unprocessed salt does not make me feel bloated or tired, while regular table salt does. Kosher salt is not necessarily unprocessed. Make sure it is unprocessed as it gives you more flavor.

Whole grains and complex carbohydrates: Whole grains are grains with their fiber and nutrients left untouched. Examples of this would be rolled oats, whole-grain flours, brown rice, sweet potatoes, and cornmeal. Whole-grain flours, like whole-gain spelt, brown rice, or whole wheat are examples of whole flours. The more natural the color, the better. If you make a chocolate cake, you may notice a slight texture change with whole-grain flours. I enjoy them anyway. For lighter treats, we need minimally refined flours, so unbleached white flour is better than bleached and a 50/50 blend of whole-grain and white flour is best. The more whole-grain flour you use, the darker your recipe will look, just as unrefined sugar makes a recipe darker. The Boston Cream Pie (see photo insert) was made with whole-grain spelt flour. (Spelt flour is a good alternative to wheat flour for those sensitive to wheat.) Baking times may vary slightly when using some whole-grain flours, so always use the toothpick test to check when your cake is done. The more whole-grain flour you use, the more grainy the recipe's texture. That is why a 50/50 blend is good, because you get more fiber but maintain a smoother texture.

Chocolate: I could write about chocolate all day. Many of the recipes call for cocoa or chocolate chips. I am a dark chocolate fan and always have been. When possible, I suggest dry powdered cocoa because I get to choose the sweetener and fat that it is dissolved in. When I buy a 70 percent cocoa bar, really dark chocolate, that means that the other 30 percent is fat and sugar that someone else chose. If I buy a bar that says 50 percent, that means that half of the bar is fat and sugar that someone else chose. Often, they are using the least expensive fat and sugar, not the one that is best for my body. When we list chocolate chips, there are several varieties for you to choose from. You should eliminate all trans fats from your house and that includes your chocolate chips. You can use up what you have, but replace them with chocolate chips that don't have any trans fats. If you want the next step up, get a chocolate chip that only has cocoa butter as the fat and uses evaporated cane juice as the sugar. This is a pretty natural, high quality chip. Another version of chocolate chip is a grain sweetened. These are sweetened with a mixture of corn and barley malt. They taste less sweet than a regular chocolate chip and also feel a little gooier in the mouth. You may love them or prefer a more traditional sweet chip. So, when I list chocolate chips, you choose what type to use and enjoy!

Water: You have to decide if your tap water is something you feel good about. If you want to improve the water you drink and cook with, you can get a filter for your faucet or the water pitchers that filter batches of water. Buying bottled water is expensive. I love the tap water I grew up with and now drink mostly filtered water for the taste.

OTHER INGREDIENTS

There are some other ingredients in the book that are found in various degrees of quality. While you can buy the generic store brand or use a more common type, in most cases the recipe will suffer: it won't taste as good and won't be as good for you. Always try to find the most organic and natural ingredients.

This cookbook is going to work like my mom's cooking. We'll make chocolate chip cookies, apple crisp, or lemon ice cream, but you'll notice small differences: "Oh, there is no sugar; it calls for honey or agave syrup."

The basic principles I am going to use in this book will ensure that you end up with a great-tasting treat, using ingredients that are better for your body. And as you cook along with me, you will learn this same fun skill while enjoying the same absolute favorite recipes that my family has enjoyed for years.

Let's get cooking!

Ingredient Substitutions

MILK SUBSTITUTION: Try substituting coconut, soy, rice, or almond milk to make a dairy-free product.

FLOUR: To thicken a recipe without flour, use cornstarch or arrowroot. If a recipe calls for 2 tablespoons of flour, substitute 1 tablespoon of cornstarch. If you are on a gluten-free diet and want to bake a cake or make cookies, substitute a commercial gluten-free baking flour or try my Gluten-Free Flour Mix (page 66). You may have to lower the oven temperature and bake for a little longer for the texture to be okay.

Vegetarian, Vegan, and Gluten Free

Almost all the recipes are vegetarian, except Hot Banana Split S'mores, Christmas Stollen, English Muffin or Pita Pizza, Leftover Pasta Frittata, Sweet Potato Pancakes, The Best Barbeque Sauce, and Wholesome Quesadilla. Throughout, some of the recipes can be either vegetarian (if using diary or honey as your sweetener) or vegan (if using egg substitute, agave syrup, maple syrup, or plant-based milks). Most of the recipes in this book are gluten free and even many of the pies can be gluten free if you choose one of the gluten-free piecrusts.

Part 2: RECIPES

CHAPTER 3
Granola,
Cereals, Trail Mixes,
and Candy

During the planning of this cookbook, I was at my mother's house in Maine. One morning at breakfast I smelled chocolate on my mother's breath and it was only 9 a.m.! My mother has been known to qualify some days as one or two chocolate square days, and especially challenging days as three-square days. That means she eats three small squares of a one-pound bar of dark chocolate. When I mentioned it, she replied with a smile, "Chocolate isn't just for breakfast anymore." My theme of this cookbook is: Dessert isn't just for dessert anymore, and comfort foods are okay!

Growing up in Maine, my mom would keep an emergency supply of water and trail mix in the trunk of her car since snowstorms were a regular event during the winter and a car getting stuck was a real possibility. Keeping some trail mix in your car, purse, or your kid's backpack is a good idea in case you get stuck without access to food. I think of trail mix as having three components: fruit, nuts, and grains. Trail mixes containing grains are granola mixed with other items like nuts, dried pineapple, or candied ginger. Not all trail mixes contain the granola component. It is easy to make (only requires baking if you add homemade granola) and is easy to transport almost anywhere, even for plane trips. Trail mix is good to have around because it combines the healthy fats and proteins found in nuts with the wholesome carbohydrates found in dried fruits and grains. It is also fairly durable in that you can carry a bag of it around without it spoiling over night, hence its name, something that it is suitable for hikers. With trail mix, the question is what do *you* like? What fruits? What nuts? Do you like small or big chunks? Chewy, crispy, or a mixture? Does adding a little chocolate or dried blueberries make you feel happy? The possibilities are endless.

I love sweet snacks that I can carry with me all day long. How many of us have spent a large amount of money for a protein bar, only to find it is too sweet? Or found that every trail mix in the store has one thing in it that you don't like and so you have to eat around it? What can we take in the car for a pick-me-up for us or the kids? And how do we address every kid's favorite category and every parent's biggest challenge: candy? This chapter will help you create your own protein bars, granola, trail mixes, and candy that will satisfy the kid and sweet tooth in all of us. How exciting to enjoy some granola just the way you like or a piece of guilt-free candy! We will help with portion control, as many of the recipes in this chapter can be made into small bite-size morsels and frozen or set aside for later, so there is just enough to savor.

GRANOLA and CEREALS

Cranberry-Walnut Granola

Honey Toasted Granola

Oatmeal Chocolate Chip Granola Bars

Peanut Butter and Jelly Granola

Three-Nut Protein Granola

Tropical High Fiber Granola

Chocolate Oatmeal

Perfect Oatmeal

. . . .

TRAIL MIXES

Banana Chocolate Chip Trail Mix

Breakfast Trail Mix

Five-Fruit Trail Mix

Four-Nut Trail Mix

Fruit-and-Nut Trail Mix

On-Time Trail Mix

Piña Colada Trail Mix

Rainbow Trail Mix

Very Berry Trail Mix

. . . .

CANDY

Almond Bark

Chocolate Oatmeal Fudge

Coconut Chocolate Holiday Eggs

Haystacks

Honey Almond Protein Bars

Hot Banana Split S'mores

Maple Sugar

Potato Candy

Stuffed Dates

～⁀CRANBERRY-WALNUT GRANOLA⁀～

I grew up eating homemade granola that my mom made for us and have found that having a tart fruit in the granola gives it extra pizzazz. I enjoy the cranberry-walnut combination. Walnuts have healthy oils and are so good for us. The protein and fat combination of the nut helps to make the granola more filling, providing lasting energy. Granola takes a little while to bake and makes your entire house smell good. This is a good granola for breakfast.

Preheat the oven to 325°F. Grease a shallow 14 x 11-inch pan with cooking spray or butter.

Combine the oats, walnuts, sesame seeds, orange zest, sugar, and salt. Mix well.

Combine the honey and oil in a separate bowl and pour over the dry ingredients. Mix well and spoon into the prepared pan.

Bake for 30 minutes, turning the pan and stirring every 10 minutes, or until golden brown.

Remove from the oven. Stir in the dried cranberries and allow to cool.

VARIATION: For Blueberry-Cranberry Granola, add ½ cup of dried blueberries at the same time you add the cranberries.

NOTE: Fruit needs to be added to granola after the baking is done. If not, it will dry out the fruit and make it tough to chew and less flavorful.

Yield: 6 cups

4 cups rolled oats

1 cup coarsely chopped walnuts

½ cup sesame seeds

2 teaspoons finely grated orange zest

¼ cup evaporated cane juice crystals

2 teaspoons unprocessed sea salt

⅔ cup honey or maple syrup

½ cup expeller-pressed oil

½ cup dried cranberries

⌒ HONEY TOASTED GRANOLA ⌒

Yield: 6 cups

4 cups rolled oats

1 cup raw almonds

½ cup pumpkin seeds

½ cup raw sunflower seeds

2 teaspoons unprocessed sea salt

¼ cup evaporated cane juice crystals

⅔ cup honey

½ cup expeller-pressed oil

Sometimes we want a classic granola recipe without any fanfare that simply tastes great. Even though it seems basic, it ends up glistening as if kissed by honey and has the perfect balance of sweet and crunchy. (See first photo insert.)

Preheat the oven to 325°F. Grease a shallow 14 x 11-inch pan with cooking spray or butter. (If you prefer granola bars that can be snacks on the go, cook it on greased parchment paper and do not stir.)

Combine the oats, almonds, pumpkin seeds, sunflower seeds, salt, and sugar. Mix well.

Combine the honey and oil in a separate bowl and pour over the dry ingredients. Mix well and spoon into the prepared pan, firmly patting the mixture to the edges.

Bake for 30 minutes, turning the pan and stirring every 10 minutes, or until golden brown.

Remove from the oven and let cool before cutting into bars, if desired.

Measuring Sticky Ingredients
Whenever you have a gooey liquid, like honey, molasses or agave syrup, and an oil to be measured, use the measuring cup to first measure the needed oil. The sticky or gooey liquid will slide out easily without much help from a rubber spatula.

Yogurt Granola
When you need a quick breakfast or lunch, yogurt granola is a great solution. Combine ⅔ cup of any of the granolas in this section with ⅓ cup unsweetened yogurt and ⅓ cup cut-up fruit. It will be a terrific fast treat.

OATMEAL CHOCOLATE CHIP GRANOLA BARS

Chocolate chips make just about everything better.

If you want a granola that has a touch of dessert to it, enjoy
this one using your favorite chocolate chips.

Preheat the oven to 325°F. Line a shallow 14 x 11-inch pan with parchment paper and grease the parchment with cooking spray or butter.

Combine the oats, pumpkin seeds, sunflower seeds, sugar, and salt. Mix well.

Combine the honey and oil in a separate bowl and pour over the dry ingredients. Mix well and spoon into the prepared pan, firmly patting the mixture to the edges.

Bake for 30 minutes, turning the pan every 10 minutes.

Remove from the oven and sprinkle the chocolate chips over the hot granola to melt. Allow to cool before cutting. Use a knife to gentle spread the melted chocolate chips.

Yield: 6 cups

5 cups rolled oats

½ cup pumpkin seeds

½ cup raw sunflower seeds

¼ cup evaporated cane juice crystals

2 teaspoons unprocessed sea salt

⅔ cup honey

½ cup expeller-pressed oil

¾ cup chocolate chips, sweetened with grain or evaporated cane juice

Kids in the Kitchen

Every parent has to decide when a child is ready to help in the kitchen. At the age of two my mom put a chair up against the counter and I would help her. The first time that I cracked an egg, I tapped the egg against the edge of the counter. The egg splattered all over the floor.

Kids love to help, yet teaching them takes additional time and patience. The benefits are family togetherness, teaching valuable life and math skills, and conveying food awareness and health lessons. Here's a secret: When kids help make something, they can't resist trying it and they often end up liking it. One way to raise kids who will make healthier choices is to have them help more in the kitchen.

∾ PEANUT BUTTER ∾
AND JELLY GRANOLA

Yield: 6 cups

4 cup rolled oats

1 cup raw peanuts

½ cup raw sesame
   seeds

½ cup raw sunflower
   seeds

¼ cup evaporated
   cane juice crystals

2 teaspoons
   unprocessed sea salt

⅔ cup fruit-sweetened
   strawberry jam

½ cup expeller-pressed
   oil

I know that my mom made this for us when she was in a hurry making our lunches. Most of us enjoy this combination and have not tasted it in a granola. It is delicious. Peanut butter and strawberry just go together. This favorite is excellent for breakfast or granola bars.

Preheat the oven to 325°F. Grease a shallow 14 x 11-inch pan with cooking spray or butter. (If you prefer granola bars that can be snacks on the go, cook it on greased parchment paper and do not stir.)

Combine the oats, peanuts, sesame seeds, sunflower seeds, sugar, and salt. Mix well.

Combine the jam and oil in a separate bowl and pour over the dry ingredients. Mix well and spoon into the prepared pan, firmly patting the mixture to the edges.

Bake for 30 minutes, turning the pan and stirring every 10 minutes, or until golden brown.

Remove from the oven and allow to cool before cutting into bars, if desired.

Working with Granola

Granola gets broken up when you stir it. So, if you want bigger chunks, don't stir it while baking. After cooling in the pan for 20 minutes, cut the granola into bars using a knife or break into large chunks. It is difficult to make granola bars with fruit since you cannot stir the granola and, therefore, cannot stir in the fruit at the end without risking breaking up the bars. Resting the fruit on the top does not work either because it will not stick to the granola.

～❂ THREE-NUT PROTEIN GRANOLA ❂～

If you love nuts and want more protein in your granola, try this recipe. We cut back on the oats and add a mixture of nuts and seeds.

Yield: 6 cups

3 cups rolled oats

1 cup raw almonds

1 cup raw cashews

1/2 cup chopped walnuts

1/2 cup raw sunflower seeds

1/4 cup evaporated cane juice crystals

2 teaspoons unprocessed sea salt

2/3 cup honey

1/2 cup expeller-pressed oil

Preheat the oven to 325°F. Grease a shallow 14 x 11-inch pan with cooking spray or butter. (If you prefer granola bars that can be snacks on the go, cook it on greased parchment paper and do not stir.)

Combine the oats, almonds, cashews, walnuts, sunflower seeds, sugar, and salt.

Combine the honey and oil in a separate bowl and pour over the dry ingredients. Mix well and spoon into the prepared pan, firmly patting the mixture to the edges.

Bake for 30 minutes, turning the pan and stirring every 10 minutes.

Remove from the oven and allow to cool before cutting into bars, if desired.

VARIATION: Substitute 1/2 cup walnuts with 1/2 cup soy nuts for a soy-based granola.

Greasing a Pan

Greasing the pan is important so that whatever you are baking doesn't stick to the pan. (I even grease wax or parchment paper because I don't like it when things stick.) My mom keeps a pastry brush in a plastic bag in the freezer. The brush always has some oil in it, but she will brush some additional butter or oil on the pan and then return the brush to the freezer. This way she does not have to keep washing the brush in between uses. She also saves butter wrappers in the freezer in a plastic bag. These butter wrappers often have enough butter on them to grease a pan.

～ **TROPICAL HIGH FIBER** ～ GRANOLA

Yield: 6 cups

4 cups rolled oats

½ cup wheat germ

½ cup soy flakes

½ cup raw sunflower
seeds

½ cup sesame seeds

½ cup coarsely
chopped walnuts or
almonds

1 cup untoasted
unsweetened finely or
coarsely shredded
coconut

½ cup evaporated
cane juice crystals

2 teaspoons
unprocessed sea salt

1 ½ teaspoons ground
cinnamon

½ cup chopped dates

¾ cup hot water

⅔ cup honey

½ cup expeller-
pressed oil

The smell of toasting coconut will fill your home as you bake this granola. Excellent for breakfast or snack bars. Fiber is an important part of everyone's diet and this sweet granola is an excellent way to start the day.

Preheat the oven to 325°F. Grease a shallow a 14 x 11-inch pan with cooking spray or butter. (If you prefer granola pieces that can be snacks on the go, cook it on greased parchment paper and do not stir.)

Combine the oats, wheat germ, soy flakes, sunflower seeds, sesame seeds, walnuts, coconut, sugar, salt, cinnamon, and dates.

Combine the hot water, honey, and oil in a separate bowl and pour over the dry ingredients.

Mix well and spoon into the prepared pan, firmly patting the mixture to the edges.

Bake for 30 minutes, turning the pan and stirring every 10 minutes. Remove from the oven and allow to cool before cutting.

Raw Nuts in Granola

You will see that we suggest you use raw nuts and seeds for granola. This is because granola is basically taking dry ingredients like oats, seeds, and nuts, making them wet with honey and oil, and popping them in the oven to dry out again. In the process of drying out the granola into chunks, the nuts get toasted. If they are already toasted, then they will get toasted twice and may have a funny, almost burnt taste.

～CHOCOLATE OATMEAL ～

Oats are a great source of fiber.

Many traditional recipes use brown sugar, fruit or raisins.
Chocolate gives a decadent twist on this wholesome breakfast
classic. Chocolate makes just about anything better.

Combine the water or milk, oats, and sea salt in a saucepan and stir.
Bring to a boil over high heat. Cover the pan, reduce the heat to low,
and simmer until the oats are tender (5 to 25 minutes, depending on
the type of oats. Boil 2 to 4 minutes for quick oats, 15 to 20 for rolled
oats, or 30 to 40 minutes for steel-cut oats).

Add the chocolate chips and stir until melted. Add the vanilla and
honey, agave syrup, or maple syrup, if desired.

Yield: 3 servings

2 cups water or organic
milk (cow, soy or other
type)

1 cup oats (quick, rolled
or steel cut)

¾ teaspoon
unprocessed sea salt

½ cup chocolate chips,
sweetened with grain
or evaporated cane
juice

½ teaspoon vanilla
extract

2 tablespoons honey,
agave syrup, or maple
syrup (optional)

~ PERFECT OATMEAL ~

Yield: 3 servings

2 cups water or organic
milk (cow, soy or other
type)

1 cup oats (quick, rolled
or steel cut)

1½ teaspoons ground
cinnamon

¾ teaspoon
unprocessed sea salt

½ cup raisins, divided

¼ cup walnut pieces,
divided

2 tablespoons honey,
agave syrup, or maple
syrup, divided

Oatmeal is the classic breakfast for those who start their day with grains. The three types of oats I have tried are quick oats, regular rolled oats, and steel-cut oats. I prefer the steel cut. However, they take 20 to 30 minutes to cook, so I only enjoy their slight crunch if I have the time or if I precook them the night before. Most of the sweetened, packaged oatmeals are too sweet for me, and it is better for your family to sweeten them with fruit or natural syrups anyway.

Combine the water or milk, oats, cinnamon, and sea salt in a saucepan. Bring to a boil over high heat. Cover the pan, reduce the heat to low, stir and simmer until the oats are tender (5 to 25 minutes, depending on type of oats. Boil 2 to 4 minutes for quick oats, 15 to 20 minutes for rolled oats, or 30 to 40 minutes for steel-cut oats.)

Divide the oatmeal among three bowls. Sprinkle the raisins and nuts on top. Drizzle each serving with the honey, agave syrup, or maple syrup to taste.

VARIATION: For a fruit-sweetened version, substitute ⅔ cup unsweetened applesauce or ⅓ cup dates puréed with the water for the syrup.

BANANA CHOCOLATE CHIP TRAIL MIX

I love banana splits. At summer camp we'd put chocolate inside a sliced banana and wrap it in foil to heat over a fire. Banana and chocolate go so well together.

Combine the almonds, walnuts, chocolate chips, banana chips, and coconut in a storage container with a tight-fitting lid. Mix well.

Store the trail mix in the refrigerator. It will keep for up to eight weeks.

Yield: 3 cups

½ cup raw or toasted almonds

1 cup walnuts

½ cup chocolate chips, sweetened with grain or evaporated cane juice

½ cup dried banana chips

½ cup unsweetened shredded coconut curls

BREAKFAST TRAIL MIX

This recipe mixes my favorite classic granola recipe with some crunch and chew.

Combine the granola, walnuts, and raisins in a storage container with a tight-fitting lid. Mix well.

Store the trail mix in the refrigerator. It will keep for up to eight weeks.

Yield: 3 cups

2 cups Honey Toasted Granola (page 28)

½ cup raw walnuts

½ cup raisins

∿ FIVE-FRUIT TRAIL MIX ∿

Yield: 3 cups

1 cup dried apple slices

½ cup dried apricots, cut in half with kitchen shears

½ cup dried cranberries

½ cup dried papaya slices

½ cup raisins

Today we have such a huge array of dried fruits available. When I was a kid, dried apples and apricots were the only ones to be found at the grocery store. I suggested a mixture below, however, feel free to substitute your favorite dried fruits. Dried fruits are chewy and fun to eat. I usually avoid the candied or sugarcoated ones and prefer to keep it to just the natural fruit.

Cut all the dried fruit into bite-size pieces.

Combine the dried apples, apricots, cranberries, papaya, and raisins in a storage container with a tight-fitting lid. Mix well.

Store the trail mix in the refrigerator. It will keep for up to eight weeks.

Sulfured or Unsulfured Dried Fruits

Sulfur is added to dried fruits to maintain their bright color and plumpness. For example, bright orange apricots have had sulfur added, whereas the ones without sulfur are dark brown and chewier. Some people have an allergy to sulfur. To know whether or not sulfur has been added to the dried fruit, check the ingredients list. I prefer dried fruits without sulfur, but it is your choice.

～◡ FOUR-NUT TRAIL MIX ◡～

Sometimes, I am just in the mood for nuts

without any dried fruit. This is my mom's favorite combination, but feel free to substitute any nuts you prefer.

Combine the almonds, peanuts, cashews, and walnuts in a storage container with a tight-fitting lid. Mix well.

Store the trail mix in the refrigerator. It will keep for up to eight weeks.

Yield: 3 cups

1 cup raw or toasted almonds

½ cup raw or toasted peanuts

½ cup raw or toasted cashews

1 cup raw or toasted walnuts

～◡ FRUIT-AND-NUT TRAIL MIX ◡～

This is the classic trail mix you find in the store

with crunchy nuts and tart and sweet fruits. (See first photo insert.)

Cut the pineapple into bite-size pieces.

Combine the almonds, walnuts, cashews, raisins, and dried pineapple in a storage container with a tight-fitting lid. Mix well.

Store the trail mix in the refrigerator. It will keep for up to eight weeks.

Yield: 3 cups

½ cup dried pineapple

1 cup almonds, raw or toasted

½ cup raw or toasted walnuts

½ cup raw or toasted cashews

½ cup raisins

∾ ON-TIME TRAIL MIX ∾

Yield: 3 cups

2 cups Three-Nut Protein Granola (page 31)

½ cup chocolate chips, sweetened with grain or evaporated cane juice

½ cup unsweetened shredded coconut curls

½ cup dried cranberries or dried cherries

Sometimes you just have to go all day long and there is no time to take a break. This trail mix has a great blend of protein, carbohydrates, and fats that taste great. The tang of the cranberries or cherries, plus the chocolate with the sweet granola and coconut will take your mind off the non-stop day and keep you going.

Combine the Three-Nut Protein Granola, chocolate chips, coconut, and dried cranberries in a storage container with a tight-fitting lid. Mix well.

Store the trail mix in the refrigerator. It will keep for up to eight weeks.

∾ PIÑA COLADA TRAIL MIX ∾

Yield: 3 cups

½ cup dried pineapple

1 cup raw or toasted almonds

½ cup macadamia nuts

½ cup unsweetened shredded coconut curls

½ cup dried banana chips

Piña coladas remind me of vacation. Growing up in Maine, I ordered a virgin piña colada any chance I had. Pineapple is naturally sweet and tangy. The nuts and coconut make a great mix of salty and sweet. Welcome to the tropics.

Cut the dried pineapple into bite-size pieces.

Combine the almonds, macadamia nuts, dried pineapple, coconut, and dried banana in a storage container with a tight-fitting lid. Mix well.

Store the trail mix in the refrigerator. It will keep for up to eight weeks.

NOTE: Dried pineapple, papaya, and mango can be found either unsweetened or sweetened. I encourage you to use the unsweetened as they are plenty sweet without added sugar.

~ RAINBOW TRAIL MIX ~

This colorful trail mix has sweet, tart and nutty
flavors combined together to make a delicious treat.
(See first photo insert.)

Combine the almonds, walnuts, dried pineapple, cranberries, papaya, and apples in a storage container with a tight-fitting lid. Mix well.

Store the trail mix in the refrigerator. It will keep for up to eight weeks.

Yield: 3 cups

1 cup raw or toasted almonds

½ cup raw or toasted walnuts

½ cup dried pineapple

½ cup dried cranberries

½ cup dried papaya

½ cup dried apples

~ VERY BERRY TRAIL MIX ~

While I love to eat fresh berries, they are
not as sturdy as dried berries. Fresh berries are very
fragile and I need a snack I can carry in my purse.

Combine the Honey Toasted Granola, almonds, dried blueberries, strawberries, and cranberries in a storage container with a tight-fitting lid. Mix well.

Store the trail mix in the refrigerator. It will keep for up to eight weeks.

NOTE: Cranberries and other tart fruits are sweetened with either sugar or fruit juice. If you can find them, select fruit juice-sweetened dried fruits rather than ones that have sugar listed as one of the first five ingredients.

Yield: 3 cups

1 cup Honey Toasted Granola (page 28)

1 cup raw or toasted almonds

½ cup dried blueberries

½ cup dried strawberries

½ cup dried cranberries

⌒◡ ALMOND BARK ◡⌒

Yield: 1¼ pounds

16 ounces dark (70% cocoa) chocolate

1 cup roasted unsalted almonds

This is one of my mom's favorite candies to make.
Because it has nuts, she sometimes considers it okay for breakfast.
She usually keeps some in her purse, and will often tuck a small
bag of it tied with a bow into gift bags. When she and her
brother and sisters went blueberry picking with their dad,
he would bring chocolate along to give to them as a treat.
In our family, chocolate is part of the love.

Line a 15 x 10-inch baking sheet with parchment paper.

In a heavy saucepan, melt the chocolate over low heat, stirring constantly. Remove the pan from the heat and add the almonds, stirring to coat.

Pour the chocolate mixture onto the prepared pan, spreading to cover the entire surface. Set aside to cool. When firm, break the bark into pieces.

⌒◡ CHOCOLATE ◡⌒
OATMEAL FUDGE

This is a way to get that fudge feeling while eating something wholesome at the same time. It feels completely decadent and is easy to store in the fridge for lunch box treats.

Grease an 8-inch square pan with cooking spray or butter.

Combine the cane juice, cocoa powder, butter, salt, and milk in a saucepan over high heat. Bring to a rolling boil and immediately remove from the stove. Add the oats, walnuts, if using, and vanilla and beat for 2 minutes with an electric mixer on low speed, or mix by hand.

Pour the fudge into the prepared pan and let cool before cutting into squares.

Yield: 8 servings

$^3/_4$ cup whole cane juice

$^1/_2$ cup cocoa powder, sifted

$^1/_2$ stick ($^1/_4$ cup) organic salted butter

$^1/_2$ teaspoon unprocessed sea salt

$^1/_2$ cup organic milk

$2^1/_2$ cups quick-cooking rolled oats

$^3/_4$ cup coarsely chopped walnuts (optional)

1 teaspoon vanilla extract

ᓚ COCONUT CHOCOLATE ᓚ
HOLIDAY EGGS

Yield: 2 dozen

1 ½ sticks (¾ cup) salted organic butter, at room temperature

1 ½ cups powdered sugar

4 cups finely grated fresh coconut

1 cup finely chopped walnuts

¼ cup half-and-half or light cream

2 teaspoons vanilla extract

8 ounces sweetened chocolate for dipping (see note)

These freshly grated coconut chocolates are labor intensive but worth it. The rich chocolate coats the white coconut filling laden with finely chopped nuts.

In a large bowl, beat the butter with an electric mixer on low speed until creamy. Add the powdered sugar, coconut, walnuts, half-and-half, and vanilla and beat until very light. Cover and let sit at room temperature for a week to "ripen". (This can be done overnight if in a pinch.)

Line a baking sheet with wax paper.

Shape the mixture into small "eggs" using a level tablespoon measure for each one. Place on the baking sheet and freeze until firm, 20 to 30 minutes.

Melt the chocolate in a double boiler over medium heat.

Insert a toothpick into the frozen "egg" and dip into the melted chocolate, using a spoon to help coat the egg. With the coated egg still on the toothpick, gently tap the toothpick on the edge of the saucepan to remove any excess chocolate. Place the egg back on the baking sheet and refrigerate until cool.

Chocolate

I prefer chocolate that is at least 70% cocoa because that means over two thirds of what you are eating is chocolate and the rest is sugar and oil. The other thing to look for is how the chocolate is sweetened. I recommend buying chocolate that is naturally sweetened. You can get grain-sweetened chocolate, whole cane sugar–sweetened chocolate, or fruit-sweetened chocolate from your local health food store.

◦◦ HAYSTACKS ◦◦

These basic chocolate and coconut candies are the right bite-size morsels to satisfy a chocolate lover. This is my kind of recipe with only two ingredients. (See first photo insert.)

Line a baking sheet with wax paper.

In a heavy saucepan, melt the chocolate over low heat. Add the coconut and stir until coated. Remove from the heat and let cool at room temperature until lukewarm.

Drop the mixture by rounded teaspoonfuls onto the prepared baking sheet. Refrigerate for at least 1 hour before eating.

Yield: 2 dozen

½ pound dark (70% cocoa) chocolate (see Better Ingredients, page 20)

¼ to ½ cup shredded dried coconut

∿ HONEY ALMOND PROTEIN BARS ∿

Yield:

4 to 8 servings

½ cup unsweetened shredded coconut

1 cup unsweetened almond (or any nut) butter, smooth or crunchy

⅓ cup honey

A great substitute for a protein bar,

these can be made as egg-size balls for a light snack or larger bars for a more significant treat.

Line a baking sheet with wax paper.

Pour the coconut into a soup bowl. In a separate bowl combine the almond butter and honey together.

Place a small amount of oil on your fingers to prevent the mixture from sticking. Shape the almond butter mixture into 1-inch balls or small rectangles. Roll the balls or rectangles in the coconut to coat and place on the prepared baking sheet. Chill in the refrigerator for at least 1 hour and then place in a storage container in the refrigerator.

Wrap the balls or bars individually with plastic wrap or place in sandwich bags to take on the go.

∽◡ HOT BANANA SPLIT S'MORES ◡∼

This is a camping treat that can be made on the back barbeque or in the oven. It is fun for kids and adults alike to make their own.

Yield:

4 servings

4 bananas, unpeeled

½ cup chocolate chips, sweetened with grain or evaporated cane juice

½ cup all-natural miniature marshmallows (optional)

Heat a grill to medium or the oven to 350°F.

Cut each unpeeled banana in half lengthwise, being careful not to cut all the way through. Carefully place about 2 tablespoons of the chocolate chips and the marshmallows in each banana. Wrap the bananas in aluminum foil squares and seal.

Bake or grill for 10 to 15 minutes, or until the chocolate and marshmallows are melted.

Serve plain or with Natural Whipped Cream (page 102) or Vanilla Ice Cream (page 109).

～◡ MAPLE SUGAR ◡～

Yield:
4 to 6 servings

1 cup maple syrup
2 teaspoons butter

In the northeast, they sell maple sugar formed into maple leaves or other shapes. My sisters and I used to tap our maple tree in the spring and collect the sap. Maple syrup comes from boiling down the sap from maple trees. The sugar comes from cooking down the syrup, and it is a traditional treat. This is a trickier recipe and I spent hours as a teenager burning the maple syrup by accident or not cooking it long enough to get the solid crystals—or forgetting to stir it and getting hard candy. You may want to start with a half or even quarter batch to start, so you can get the feel of it. If you burn it or it doesn't come out right the first time, try again. It always works; you just have to get the feel of it. You are boiling off water to the point it can crystallize. Eating the mistakes is also fun! (See first photo insert.)

Grease one 6-cup muffin tin .

Cook the syrup over medium heat until boiling, stirring constantly. Once boiling, reduce to low heat and simmer. You will know you are getting close when it gets foamy. For a full batch, this can take anywhere from 10 to 20 minutes depending on your stove.

When the heated syrup is thick enough to make a "thread" when the spoon is pulled out, remove the syrup from the heat and add the butter. (I keep scooping syrup in a spoon and pouring it back into the pot. As the syrup gets thicker, the stream of syrup gets thicker and moves more slowly. At some point, the syrup will almost stop mid pour and solidify into a small sugar thread.)

Remove from the heat and stir quickly until the clear syrup starts to become opaque and crystallize. If it takes more than 5 to 7 minutes to become opaque, place it back on the stove and boil again for a minute or two, testing the thread and boiling off just a little more water. Remove from the stove again and stir until crystallized.

As soon as it begins to crystallize, scoop the syrup into the muffin cups. Set the pan in the refrigerator to cool.

These disks can be broken and served in chunks.

NOTE: You can also use molds, a mini muffin tin, or even greased wax paper if you don't have a muffin pan.

⌒◡ **POTATO CANDY** ◡⌒

When I was a child, we made this candy at

Thanksgiving and Christmas. I liked it because I could help when
I was little and there were lots of fun parts to it. I could mix and roll out
the batter, spread the peanut butter, roll it up, and, when I got older,
cut it into pieces. I was fascinated by the swirls of peanut butter and
that I had made something so cool. This can be made with any nut
butter, from almond to soy. It looks like a cinnamon roll; the "bun"
part is the potato and the "cinnamon" part is peanut butter.
Pretty pinwheels. (See first photo insert.)

Yield: 6 dozen

2 teaspoons organic
butter

1 teaspoon vanilla
extract

½ cup cooked
mashed potato

4½ cups organic
powered sugar, sifted

2 cups peanut butter,
fresh ground or
unsweetneed from
a jar

Combine the butter, vanilla, and mashed potato in a bowl and mix
well. Add the powdered sugar and mix until very thick, almost like
pastry dough, adding more sugar if necessary.

Dust a sheet of wax paper with powdered sugar. Place the dough on
the wax paper and roll it out into a rectangular piecrust, approximately 10 x 12 inches.

Spread the peanut butter over the dough to $\frac{1}{8}$- to $\frac{1}{4}$-inch thick, cov-
ering the entire surface. Roll up lengthwise like a jellyroll, and chill in
the refrigerator for 1 to 2 hours.

Slice into $\frac{1}{4}$-inch pieces and serve.

∼◡ STUFFED DATES ◡∼

This is a great recipe to have kids help with.

My mom had us helping her with this as kids and we loved making these. They are in the candy category because they are as good as candy.

Cut a small slit in each date and stuff with 1 or 2 walnut quarters, depending on the size of the date.

Roll in the coconut if desired.

Yield:

6 servings

2 dozen dates, pitted

2 dozen walnut halves, cut in half lengthwise

½ cup unsweetened shredded coconut (optional)

CHAPTER 4
Cakes, Muffins, Frosting, and Fillings

Cakes can be dense, rich, light, fruity, or chocolaty or a combination. In our family, my mom made each of our favorite cakes for our birthdays. My dad always picked a Boston Cream Pie and I picked a funny chocolate cake with custard and homemade marshmallow frosting. Muffins are mini cakes to take with us on the go. And what would cakes be without something on top? I know that frostings are stretching the wholesome junk food theme, yet we all need treats from time to time. I'd say my favorite recipe in this entire chapter is the fluffy marshmallow frosting. Have fun; enjoy the cakes and muffins here.

Baking Cakes

A cake needs to be timed correctly, for if it bakes too long it will be dry, and if you take it out before it's done, it will be doughy in the middle and may collapse. To assure that a cake is done, you need a toothpick or a piece of dried spaghetti. Pull the oven rack out and insert the toothpick or spaghetti into the center of the cake down to the bottom and then remove it. If the toothpick comes out clean, then you have a done cake. If it comes out with batter, the cake needs to bake more until the toothpick comes out clean. Everyone's oven is different so even if your cake is a nice light brown color and is beautifully raised, take the time to check the center. It is disappointing to do all the work and have a problem at the end. Keep in mind that whole-grain flours will cause your cake to be darker and have a more grainy texture. The whole-grain flours can also add time to your baking and require a slightly lower temperature, which makes the toothpick test so important. I recommend a 50/50 blend of unbleached white flour and whole-grain flour for lighter, fluffier cakes with more fiber.

CAKES

Boston Cream Pie

Christmas Stollen

Cinnamon Buns

Grandma's Gingerbread Cake

Lemon Pound Cake

One Pan Eggless Chocolate Cake

Scotch Scones

Walnut Applesauce Cake

• • • • • • • • • • • • •

MUFFINS

Almond Energy Muffins

Apple and Date Gluten-Free Muffins

Cashew Protein Muffins

Chocolate-Zucchini Muffins

Gluten-Free Flour Mix

Golden Pineapple-Carrot Muffins

Hazelnut Protein Muffins

• • • • • • • • • • • • •

FROSTING and FILLINGS

Chocolate Ganache

Chocolate Non-Butter Cream Frosting

Custard Filling

Fluffy Marshmallow Frosting

❦ BOSTON CREAM PIE ❧

Yield:

6 to 8 servings

2 eggs

1 teaspoon vanilla extract

1 cup evaporated cane juice

1 cup sifted unbleached wheat or spelt flour

1 teaspoon baking powder

1/4 teaspoon unprocessed sea salt

1/2 cup plus 2 tablespoons organic milk, divided

2 tablespoons organic butter or expeller-pressed oil

Custard Filling (page 70)

1/2 cup chocolate chips, sweetened with grain or evaporated cane juice

My sisters and I always made this cake for my dad's birthday since this was his favorite cake. It was confusing to me that it was called a pie when it was really a cake. This is a basic cake with a light custard filling topped with a thin coat of chocolate, almost like an éclair, but a cake. (See first photo insert.)

Preheat the oven to 350°F. Grease an 8-inch round pan.

Beat the eggs and vanilla in a mixing bowl until thick and creamy. Gradually add the evaporated cane juice and beat until incorporated.

In a separate bowl, sift together the flour, baking powder, and salt. Add the dry ingredients to the egg mixture.

Heat 1/2 cup of the milk and the butter in a medium saucepan just to the boiling point. Add to the flour mixture and mix to form a batter.

Spread the batter into the prepared pan and bake for 30 to 40 minutes, or until a toothpick inserted into the center of the cake comes out clean. Remove from the oven and allow to cool.

When the cake has cooled, carefully cut it in half horizontally using a serrated knife and remove the top layer, using a wide spatula.

Spread the Custard Filling over the bottom layer and replace the top layer.

In a saucepan, melt the chocolate chips with the remaining 2 tablespoons of milk over medium-low heat. Spread the melted chocolate on the top of the cake and serve.

Removing Cakes from Pans

Nonstick pans work fairly well; however, I like to add a little shortening and flour to them, as the cakes can get stuck. Regular pans that are not nonstick require more set up to assure that the cake will come out. Complicated shapes, like a Bundt cake, need to be rubbed generously with butter or a non-dairy butter-like substance, then coated with the flour you are using in the recipe. For regular cake pans and whenever possible, I prefer to use wax or parchment paper. I place the cut paper in the pan, then take a small amount of oil, butter, or non-dairy healthy spread and rub it with my fingers to coat it. After the cake is cooled, I take a wooden knife if it is a nonstick pan or a regular knife if it is a regular pan and cut around the edges, loosening them. I then place a cooling rack on the top of the cake, and flip it gently. The cake will fall right out, as the wax paper has prevented any sticking from happening.

Custom Fitting Wax Paper

Turn the pan upside down and place a piece of wax paper big enough to cover it on top. Use your fingernail or a wooden spoon to rub the edges of the pan, tracing the shape by making a mark on the wax paper. Then, cut the wax paper in the shape of the pan you just traced. Voilà! Your pan is fitted.

∾ CHRISTMAS STOLLEN ∾

Yield: 2 loaves

1/4 cup chopped citron

1/4 cup chopped candied orange peel

1/4 cup golden raisins

1/4 cup dried cranberries

1/3 cup rum

1 cup lukewarm (105°F to 110°F) organic milk

1 tablespoon active dry yeast

4 cups sifted unbleached flour, divided

2 sticks (1 cup) organic butter, at room temperature

1/2 cup honey

2 eggs

1/2 teaspoon almond extract

1 cup mashed potato

2 teaspoons unprocessed sea salt

Zest of 1 lemon

1/2 cup almonds, chopped

1/2 teaspoon mace

There are many jokes about holiday fruit cakes because they traditionally do not taste that good. This one is an exception. Since I was a child, I have enjoyed this traditional holiday bread. It is a yeast bread with all sorts of fun flavors in it—but without too much going on. Enjoy this family favorite.

Grease a large baking sheet.

In a bowl, soak the citron, orange peel, raisins, and cranberries in the rum for 1 hour.

Combine the warm milk, yeast, and 1 cup of the flour in a mixing bowl. Beat well and let stand in a warm place until light and fluffy, about 1 hour.

In a separate mixing bowl, beat the butter until creamy. Add the honey and mix well. Set aside 2 tablespoons of the butter-honey mixture for brushing the tops of loaves. Beat in the eggs one at a time. Add the almond extract. Add the yeast mixture, mashed potato, salt, lemon zest, almonds, and soaked fruit mixture.

Sift the mace, cinnamon, and nutmeg into a separate bowl. Sift 2 cups of the flour into the mace mixture and mix well. Add the dry ingredients to the fruit mixture and mix well. Add enough additional flour to make a dough that is soft but not sticky.

Knead the dough on a lightly floured board until smooth and elastic, 8 to 10 minutes, adding flour as needed. Return the dough to the bowl, cover, and let rise for 1 1/2 hours, or until doubled in bulk. Punch down the dough and shape into two balls; let rest for 10 minutes.

Flatten each ball into an oval about 3/4 inch thick. Brush with the melted butter and fold nearly in half. Place on the prepared baking sheet and brush the tops with the reserved butter-honey mixture. Let

½ teaspoon ground
  cinnamon

½ teaspoon ground
  nutmeg

2 tablespoons butter,
  melted

2 tablespoons
  powdered sugar
  for dusting

rise until doubled in bulk, around 1 hour.

Preheat the oven to 350°F and bake for 35 to 40 minutes. Remove from the oven to cool. When cool, dust with powdered sugar.

～ CINNAMON BUNS ～

Yield:

15 to 18 servings

2 teaspoons (1 package) active dry yeast

1 cup lukewarm (105°F to 110°F) organic milk

½ cup expeller-pressed canola or sunflower oil

¼ cup honey

2 eggs

1 cup whole wheat flour

1½ teaspoons unprocessed sea salt

2 to 3 cups unbleached flour, sifted, divided

½ cup salted organic butter, at room temperature

½ cup evaporated cane sugar

1 teaspoon ground cinnamon

½ cup finely chopped walnuts (optional)

½ cup raisins (optional)

A childhood friend asked me, "Are you going to include a cinnamon roll recipe in your cookbook? I want to make them for my kids, but a healthier version." This was one of my favorite breakfast treats growing up: the warm bread wrapped around the sweet and sticky cinnamon. These are great sources of fiber and also are accented with just enough sweetness.

Grease a baking sheet.

Mix the yeast and milk together in a small bowl.

In a mixing bowl, cream the oil and honey together. Add the eggs one at a time, beating after each addition. Add the yeast mixture, whole wheat flour, and salt, beating well. Add 2 cups of the unbleached flour and beat until smooth. Add enough additional unbleached flour to make a dough that is soft but not sticky.

Knead the dough on a lightly floured board until it is smooth and elastic, 8 to 10 minutes, adding flour as needed.

Return to the bowl, cover and let rise for 1 to 1½ hours, or until doubled in bulk.

Roll into a rectangle until the dough is about ½ inch thick. Spread the softened butter over the dough. Combine the sugar and cinnamon together in a bowl and sprinkle evenly over the butter. Sprinkle with the nuts and raisins if desired.

Starting with the long edge, roll the dough snugly into a log, pressing the edge to seal.

With the seam side down, cut the dough crosswise into 1-inch slices and arrange on the prepared baking sheet. Cover and let rise until doubled in bulk, 30 to 45 minutes.

Preheat the oven to 375°F. Bake for 20 minutes, or until light golden brown.

~ GRANDMA'S ~ GINGERBREAD CAKE

This is my grandmother's gingerbread cake with a little less molasses than she used. It is moist and gooey and has a nice blend of spices. I remember baking this with my mom when I was little.

Preheat the oven to 350°F. Grease a 9-inch square baking pan (with or without wax paper). Dust with flour.

Sift the flour, cinnamon, ginger, baking soda, and salt into a bowl; set aside.

Combine the eggs and buttermilk in a large bowl and beat until well mixed.

Heat the oil and molasses in a saucepan over medium heat just to boiling and remove from the heat. Add the molasses mixture to the egg mixture alternately with dry ingredients.

Pour into the prepared pan and bake until a toothpick inserted into the center of the cake comes out clean, about 20 to 25 minutes. Cool the cake in the pan for 15 minutes, then invert onto a wire rack to cool completely.

My grandmother served with this cake Fluffy Marshmallow Frosting (page 71), but I like it topped with Natural Whipped Cream (page 102) or ice cream.

Yield:
9 servings

1¾ cups unbleached wheat or spelt flour

2 teaspoons ground cinnamon

1 teaspoon ground ginger

2 teaspoons baking soda

½ teaspoon unprocessed sea salt

2 eggs

½ cup buttermilk (or ½ cup milk plus 1½ teaspoons vinegar or lemon juice)

½ cup expeller-pressed oil

⅔ cup molasses

∿LEMON POUND CAKE ∿

2 sticks (1 cup) butter, at room temperature

¾ cup evaporated cane sugar, sifted

5 eggs

2 teaspoons lemon extract

Zest of one organic lemon, or 1 teaspoon

2 cups unbleached flour, sifted then measured

1 teaspoon baking powder

1½ teaspoons unprocessed sea salt

Pound cake is often made with eggs as the only leavening. We found that when the amount of sugar is reduced and the kind of sugar is changed, additional leavening creates a finer texture. (See first photo insert.)

Preheat the oven to 350°F. Grease a loaf pan and line the bottom with wax paper.

Beat the butter and sugar together in a mixing bowl until light and fluffy. Add the eggs one at a time, beating after each addition. Add the lemon extract and lemon zest.

Sift the flour, baking powder, and salt together.

Add the flour mixture to the creamed mixture and beat just until smooth.

Pour into the loaf pan and bake for 1 to 1¼ hours, or until it tests done. Cool the cake in the pan for a few minutes; then turn out onto a wire rack to cool completely.

Serve plain or with Strawberry Sauce (page 112), Natural Whipped Cream (page 102), or ice cream.

ONE PAN EGGLESS CHOCOLATE CAKE

This eggless cake is called a one pan cake
because everything is mixed together in the baking pan.
It makes for easy cleanup. (See second photo insert.)

Preheat the oven to 350°F.

Stir together the spelt flour, sugar, cocoa powder, baking soda, and sea salt in an ungreased 8-inch square pan.

Add the oil, vinegar, and vanilla. Pour the water over all and mix well with a fork.

Bake for 30 to 35 minutes.

VARIATIONS: To make 14 whoopie pie halves, double the recipe except for the water. Drop ¼ cup batter on a baking sheet lined with wax paper and bake for about 20 minutes.

Yield:

9 servings

1½ cups unbleached spelt flour

½ cup whole evaporated cane sugar

4 tablespoons cocoa powder

1 teaspoon baking soda

½ teaspoon unprocessed sea salt

6 tablespoons expeller-pressed oil

2 tablespoons cider vinegar

1 teaspoon vanilla extract

1 cup water

⁓◡ SCOTCH SCONES ◡⁓

Yield: 8 scones

A delightful bread for breakfast or tea.

Using dried cranberries instead of raisins adds a tangy flavor.

2 cups spelt flour

3 teaspoons baking powder

1 teaspoon unprocessed sea salt

⅓ cup salted butter

½ cup organic milk

¼ cup honey

1 whole egg

1 egg, separated

½ cup dried cranberries

1 tablespoon evaporated cane sugar

Preheat the oven to 425°F.

Sift together the spelt flour, baking powder, and sea salt in a bowl. Cut in the butter until the mixture looks like coarse meal.

Add the milk, honey, whole egg, and egg yolk. Stir with a fork only until the flour is moistened. Add the dried cranberries.

Turn the dough out onto a floured board and knead gently for about 20 seconds. Roll into a circle about ½ inch thick.

Slightly beat the egg white with a tablespoon of water and brush the dough with the egg wash. Sprinkle with the sugar.

Cut the dough into 8 pie-shaped pieces and place on an ungreased baking sheet. Bake for 12 to 15 minutes, or until golden.

Split the scones and serve warm with butter.

~ WALNUT APPLESAUCE CAKE ~

This was the family wedding cake, and it was delicious served with a butter cream frosting. I like this cake. It is kind of neat enjoying the cake that my parents had for their wedding. This is a great cake for an afternoon snack or for breakfast.

Sift the flour, sugar, cinnamon, cloves, baking soda, and salt together in a large bowl.

In separate bowl, combine the applesauce, oil, raisins, and walnuts. Add to the dry ingredients and blend gently.

Pour the batter into a greased 8-inch square pan and bake at 350°F for 40 to 45 minutes or until a toothpick inserted into the center comes out clean.

Yield:
9 servings

1³/₄ cups spelt flour, sifted

¹/₂ cup evaporated cane sugar

¹/₂ teaspoon ground cinnamon

¹/₂ teaspoon ground cloves

1 teaspoon baking soda

¹/₄ teaspoon un-processed sea salt

1 cup unsweetened applesauce

¹/₂ cup expeller-pressed oil

1 cup raisins

1 cup walnuts

～ ALMOND ENERGY MUFFINS ～

Yield: 6 muffins

1 egg, beaten

1/3 cup expeller-
    pressed oil

1/4 cup agave syrup

2 cups almond meal

1 tablespoon baking
    powder

1/4 cup organic milk

1 teaspoon almond
    extract

1/2 teaspoon
    unprocessed
    sea salt

These dense, rich muffins use almond meal for the flour. To make the almond meal, process about eight ounces of whole raw almonds in a food processor until finely chopped. Almonds are full of protein and good fat comes rom the nuts, eggs, and oil. The agave syrup gives the muffins a slight sweetness. This is a great muffin when you need more energy, as it will provide you sustainable energy for hours. These muffins are gluten free.

Preheat the oven to 375°F. Grease a 6-cup muffin tin.

Combine the egg, oil, and agave syrup and mix well.

Add the almond meal, baking powder, milk, almond extract, and sea salt and blend just until smooth.

Fill the muffin tin cups two-thirds full using a 1/3-cup measure.

Bake for 20 to 25 minutes, or until a toothpick inserted into the center of a muffin comes out clean.

NOTE: In most muffin or quick bread recipes, you can substitute half of the flour with a whole grain equivalent. Adding more than that may change the texture significantly.

~⌣ APPLE AND DATE ⌣~ GLUTEN-FREE MUFFINS

A great breakfast muffin, we use dates for both texture and sweetener. The tart apple slices round out this nutritious and wholesome on-the-go meal.

Preheat the oven to 325°F. Grease an 8-cup muffin tin.

Combine the flour mix, salt, baking powder, and baking soda together in a large bowl.

Combine the milk, egg, oil, and whole dates in a blender and process until smooth.

Pour the wet ingredients into the dry and mix well.

Add the chopped dates and apple. Fill the muffin tin cups two-thirds full using a $1/3$-cup measure.

Bake for 20 to 25 minutes, or until golden brown at the edges and a toothpick inserted into the center of a muffin comes out clean.

NOTE: If you don't have an 8-cup muffin tin, you can use a 9-cup one, but they will be a little smaller. Begin checking them after 15 minutes as the smaller muffins won't take as long to cook.

Yield: 8 muffins

$1\frac{1}{2}$ cups Gluten-Free Flour Mix (page 66)

$\frac{1}{2}$ teaspoon unprocessed sea salt

1 teaspoon baking powder

1 teaspoon baking soda

$\frac{3}{4}$ cup organic milk

1 egg

$\frac{1}{4}$ cup expeller-pressed oil

$\frac{1}{4}$ cup whole dates

$\frac{1}{2}$ cup dates, chopped into $\frac{1}{2}$-inch pieces

1 apple, chopped into $\frac{1}{2}$-inch pieces (about 1 cup)

❧ CASHEW PROTEIN MUFFINS ❧

Yield: 6 muffins

1 egg

¼ cup expeller-
pressed oil

¼ cup agave syrup

2 cups cashew meal

1 tablespoon baking
powder

⅓ cup organic milk

1 teaspoon ground
cinnamon

½ teaspoon
unprocessed sea salt

We had some leftover cashew meal and decided to
try it for a muffin. To make the cashew meal, just blend about eight
ounces of whole raw cashews in a food processor until finely chopped. The cashews are much milder than the almonds yet are rich
and nutty in flavor. These are not light and airy but more like a bowl of
oatmeal. The hint of cinnamon and gentle sweetener blends well.

Preheat the oven to 375°F. Grease a 6-cup muffin tin.

Beat the egg in a bowl. Stir in the oil and agave syrup. Add the
cashew meal, baking powder, milk, cinnamon, and sea salt and blend
just until smooth.

Fill the muffin tin cups two-thirds full, using a ⅓-cup measure.

Bake for 20 to 25 minutes, or until a toothpick inserted into the center of a muffin comes out clean.

CHOCOLATE-ZUCCHINI MUFFINS

These taste like little chocolate cakes but are less sweet and more substantial. These make a great breakfast muffin or afternoon snack.

Preheat the oven to 400°F. Grease an 8-cup muffin tin.

Sift together the flour, cocoa powder, salt, baking soda, and baking powder in a large bowl.

Beat the eggs in a separate bowl and add the agave syrup, oil, zucchini, and vanilla.

Add the wet ingredients to the dry ingredients and stir until blended.

Fill the greased muffin tin cups two-thirds full, using a $1/3$-cup measure.

Bake for 20 minutes, or until a toothpick inserted into the center of a muffin comes out clean.

Breaking Eggs

When adding eggs to a recipe, breaking each egg individually into a small dish first allows you to check for pieces of shell or other impurities that sometimes occur in eggs.

Yield: 8 muffins

$1\frac{1}{2}$ cups unbleached flour

$\frac{1}{2}$ cup cocoa powder

1 teaspoon unprocessed sea salt

1 teaspoon baking soda

$\frac{1}{2}$ teaspoon baking powder

2 eggs

$\frac{1}{2}$ cup agave syrup

$\frac{1}{2}$ cup expeller-pressed oil

1 cup grated zucchini

1 teaspoon vanilla extract

∽◡ GLUTEN-FREE FLOUR MIX ◡∾

Yield: 4¼ cups

3 cups fine rice flour

¾ cup tapioca starch

½ cup potato starch

You can buy ready-to-use gluten-free cake or muffin flour mixes or you can make your own. Use whatever you think is best.

Combine the rice flour, tapioca starch, and potato starch in a container and store in the refrigerator.

Converting to Gluten Free

You can convert most recipes to gluten free by removing the sources of gluten, like wheat, barley, or spelt, and using the mix above. You will need to lower the oven temperature and increase the baking time, as rice flour needs to cook longer at a lower temperature.

Tip for Light Batter

Usually when baking, we think nothing of mixing the batter in a mixer for a long while. However, part of the appeal of muffins, pancakes, and batter breads is the cakey, non-chewy texture. Kneading brings out the gluten, a protein in flour, and affects the texture of baked goods. It is what makes bagels and pizza crust chewy because they are kneaded. You do not want to overmix the batter for baked goods like pancakes, muffins, and batter breads, or you will have a rubbery creation. So, when making muffins, pancakes, and batter breads, the saying is "mix just until you have barely wet the dry ingredients and stop." This will produce light and cakey treats every time.

GOLDEN PINEAPPLE-
CARROT MUFFINS

These light and cakey yet wholesome muffins are perfect for breakfast or a lunch snack. The banana and pineapple add a natural source of sweetness while the strands of grated carrot add texture and color. Enjoy warm out of the oven. (See first photo insert.)

Preheat the oven to 400°F. Grease an 8-cup muffin tin.

Sift together the flour, baking powder, baking soda, cinnamon, and salt into a large bowl.

Combine the eggs, banana, oil, and vanilla in a blender. Pour over the dry ingredients. Add the walnuts, pineapple, carrot, and nuts and stir just until the flour is moistened.

Fill the muffin tin cups two-thirds full, using a $1/3$-cup measure.

Bake for 20 minutes or until golden brown, testing for doneness with a toothpick or piece of pasta.

Yield: 8 muffins

1 1/2 cups unbleached flour

1 teaspoon baking powder

1/2 teaspoon baking soda

1 teaspoon ground cinnamon

1 teaspoon unprocessed sea salt

2 eggs

1/2 cup mashed banana

1/2 cup expeller-pressed oil

1 teaspoon vanilla extract

1/2 cup coarsely chopped walnuts

1/2 cup canned crushed unsweetened pineapple, undrained

1/2 cup finely shredded raw carrot

⌒⌣ HAZELNUT PROTEIN MUFFINS ⌣⌒

Yield: 6 muffins

1 egg

⅓ cup expeller-
 pressed oil

¼ cup agave syrup

½ cup organic milk

2 cups hazelnut meal

1 tablespoon baking
 powder

1 teaspoon
 unprocessed sea salt

⅓ cup dried
 cranberries

These nut-based muffins have a dense
and fruity taste. Filling and rich, they have the wholesome
oils from nuts and natural sweetness from agave syrup.

Preheat the oven to 375°F. Grease a muffin tin.

Beat the egg in a large bowl, then add the oil and agave syrup. Add
the milk, hazelnut meal, baking powder, sea salt, and dried cranberries and blend just until smooth.

Fill the muffin tin cups two-thirds full, using a ⅓-cup measure.

Bake for 20 to 25 minutes, or until a toothpick inserted into the center of a muffin comes out clean.

⌒⌣ CHOCOLATE GANACHE ⌣⌒

Yield: 1 cup

3 ounces dark (70%
 cocoa) chocolate,
 broken into ½-inch
 pieces

½ cup heavy cream

This is a perfect topping for
Boston Cream Pie (page 52). See first photo insert.

In a small heavy saucepan, melt the chocolate over low heat.
Remove from the heat and add the cream, stirring until blended.
Allow to cool until just warm before spreading on the cake.

CHOCOLATE NON-BUTTER CREAM FROSTING

My friend Cole likes to make birthday cakes for his friends and family. This simple recipe makes a rich chocolate frosting. I enjoy it so much that I like to leave some extra frosting in the bowl for another taste. This is perfect for cakes and cupcakes, or if you wanted to fill whoopie pies with chocolate (page 59).

Sift together the powdered evaporated cane juice and cocoa powder in a mixing bowl. Add the butter spread and blend by hand or using an electric mixer. Add the vanilla extract and mix to combine.

This is delicious on the Walnut Applesauce Cake, (page 61).

NOTE: You can use real butter instead of the vegan spread for a creamier frosting. For a plain frosting, leave out the cocoa powder and add more powdered sugar as needed.

Yield: enough to frost a 2-layer 8-inch cake

1 cup powdered evaporated cane juice

1/3 cup cocoa powder

2/3 cup vegan butter spread (Healthy Choice, Earth Balance), at room temperature

1 teaspoon vanilla extract

~⌣ CUSTARD FILLING ⌣~

Yield: 1 cup

⅓ cup organic
powdered sugar

3 tablespoons
cornstarch

⅛ teaspoon
unprocessed sea salt

1 cup scalded organic
milk

1 egg, beaten

¼ teaspoon vanilla
extract

This summer custard recipe is served by itself and
is the perfect custard for a cake filling because it spreads easily.
This is the filling for the Boston Cream Pie (see first photo
insert) and can be used with any cake

Combine the sugar, cornstarch, and salt in a heavy saucepan. Add the scalded milk, stirring constantly.

Pour half of the hot mixture into the beaten egg, stirring constantly.

Pour the egg mixture back into the saucepan and simmer for 3 to 4 minutes.

Remove from the heat and let cool to lukewarm.

Add the vanilla and stir.

Let cool completely before using as a cake filling.

⁓ FLUFFY ⁓
MARSHMALLOW FROSTING

This is a gooey homemade white frosting with the best texture. It looks like clouds and tastes light, airy, and sweet. Perfect for topping on gingerbread, filling for whoopie pies, or frosting a cake.

Yield: 1 cup

½ cup maple syrup

2 egg whites, stiffly beaten

1 teaspoon vanilla extract

⅛ teaspoon unprocessed sea salt

In a saucepan, boil the maple syrup over medium heat without stirring, for about 5 minutes. Begin testing it by stirring occasionally until a small amount spins a thread 5 to 6 inches long.

Pour the syrup in a fine stream over the stiffly beaten egg whites while beating constantly.

Add the vanilla and sea salt. Beat for 5 minutes until the frosting is the right consistency for spreading.

CHAPTER 5
Cookies, Pies, Puddings, and Toppings

This may come as no surprise to many, but this is probably my favorite chapter. After all, it does contain cookies. Growing up, I looked forward to cookies, pies, and puddings.

And, once again, we are providing you the way to bake the most fantastic and wholesome desserts. Here is the best part: so many of our treats are not just for dessert. Our pies can be enjoyed for breakfast and our cookies for an afternoon snack. Speaking of pies, ours are made with whole grain crusts, natural sweeteners, and fruit, which make them phenomenal.

When testing these recipes, I realized I had never before tasted fresh blueberry pie with uncooked blueberries. The tricky part was trying to set aside some for my sister to taste. My mom had to hide a slice for her in the fridge. It is that good!

Part of what makes pies special is that they are labor intensive. Pies are an old-fashioned dessert that can have any of a number of fillings from fruit to chocolate cream. Pies come with either one or two crusts. Two-crust pies are typically fruit pies since you want to retain the moisture. Single-crust pies are pies like pecan or unbaked pies such as pudding filled.

Crisps are similar to pies but take less work. Instead of handmade crusts on the top and bottom, crisps have the fruit filling of a pie with a crumb topping.

Puddings can either be used as a pie filling or served as a dessert on their own. We've also included some toppings that can be enjoyed on pies and other desserts. A dollop of homemade ice cream (see chapter 6) goes well on many of the pies.

COOKIES

Breakfast Macaroons

Chocolate Chip Oatmeal Cookies

Honey Cakes

Oatmeal Chocolate Chip Banana Cookies

Peppernuts

Real Ginger Cookies

Snowballs

• • • • • • • • • • • • •

PIES, SQUARES, and CRUSTS

Apple Cream Cheese Torte

Fruit Kabobs

Baked Apples

Bite-lette Apple Crisp

Blueberry Pie Perfection

Cherry Pie

Cranberry Pecan Pie

Fresh Blueberry Pie

Fresh Fruit Pizza Pie

Apple Pie

Lemon Squares

Milk Chocolate Cream Pie

Mini Pumpkin Pies

Pecan Pie

Rhubarb Pie

Rice Pie

Strawberry-Rhubarb Pie

Organic Butter Piecrust

Organic Oil Piecrust

Press-In Gluten-Free Piecrust

Laura's Wholesome Junk Food Piecrust
Roll-Out Gluten-Free Piecrust
Graham Cracker Piecrust

• • • • • • • • • • • •

PUDDINGS and TOPPINGS
Homemade Chocolate Pudding
Natural Whipped Cream
Fresh Apple Topping
Summer Vanilla Custard

∾◡ BREAKFAST MACAROONS ◡∾

Macaroons are one of my favorite treats. Since
they don't have flour, they are a great gluten-free snack. They are high
in fiber, thanks to the nutritious shredded coconut. Linda Stone created
this recipe after lots of experimenting. (See second photo insert.)

Yield: 12 macaroons

2 egg whites

1/2 teaspoon vanilla extract

1/4 teaspoon almond extract

Pinch of unprocessed sea salt

1 tablespoon evaporated cane juice

1 1/2 teaspoons agave syrup

1 1/2 teaspoons maple syrup

1 1/2 teaspoons melted coconut oil

3/4 to 1 cup finely shredded unsweetened coconut

Preheat the oven to 300°F. Grease a cookie sheet.

Combine the egg whites, vanilla extract, almond extract, salt, cane juice, agave syrup, maple syrup, and coconut oil in a mixing bowl. Beat with an electric mixer until soft peaks form.

Add the coconut very gradually, mixing until the consistency is thick enough to shape into balls without much spreading. Shape the mixture into tablespoon-size balls and carefully place on the prepared cookie sheet.

Bake for 12 to 15 minutes or until the tips are golden brown.

NOTE: You can use all vanilla and no almond extract, too.

VARIATIONS: For macaroons with miniature dark chocolate chips, partially grind about 2 ounces of dark chocolate chips in a coffee grinder, leaving some large pieces, and add with the coconut. Or add 1/2 teaspoon cocoa powder to the egg whites and, if you desire, partially ground dark chocolate chips with the coconut.

- -

Good Fat

I do not believe in the non-fat trend and have not followed it. Fat is what makes us feel full or satisfied and is an important component of our diet. What is important is to avoid trans and hydrogenated fats and to look for natural sources of nutritious fats.

- -

CHOCOLATE CHIP OATMEAL COOKIES

Yield: 4 dozen

1 stick (½ cup) salted organic butter

½ cup expeller-pressed canola or sunflower oil

3 eggs

1 cup maple syrup

1 cup whole wheat flour

1½ cups unbleached white flour

2 teaspoons baking soda

2 teaspoons unprocessed sea salt

3 cups rolled oats

1 cup coarsely chopped walnuts

¾ cup chocolate chips, sweetened with grain or evaporated cane juice

Who doesn't love chocolate chip cookies? These are good enough to have for breakfast. With whole oats and some whole grain flour, these cookies are tasty and filling. This is a version of my grandmother's recipe when cookies were both a treat and a welcomed source of energy. Enjoy these with homeade ice cream (pages 106-109), with milk, crumbled on some yogurt, or just warm out of the oven. They are out of this world. (See second photo insert.)

Preheat the oven to 375°F.

Cream the butter in a mixing bowl until light. Add the oil, eggs, and maple syrup, beating well after each addition.

In a separate bowl sift the flours, baking soda, and salt.

Gradually add the flour mixture to the creamed mixture, mixing well. If the dough seems too stiff, add 1 to 2 tablespoons of water to soften the dough.

Stir in the rolled oats. Add the walnuts and chocolate chips.

Drop by tablespoonfuls onto an ungreased cookie sheet and bake for 8 to 10 minutes, or until just light golden.

⌒◡ HONEY CAKES ◡⌒

These nut and honey cookies have a wonderful spice blend and old-world flavor. They are great for an after-school treat or to bring to a party.

Preheat the oven to 400°F. Grease a cookie sheet.

Combine the eggs and honey in a mixing bowl and beat until well mixed.

Sift the flour, baking soda, cinnamon, allspice, and cloves in a bowl. Stir in the almonds, citron, lemon extract, and salt.

Add the egg mixture to the flour mixture and mix well.

Roll the dough onto a floured surface to $^1\!/_4$-inch thickness. Cut with a round cookie cutter and place on the prepared cookie sheet. Bake for 12 to 15 minutes, or just until golden brown.

NOTE: You can roll out the dough, wrap in plastic, and store in the refrigerator to use later. When ready, allow the dough to come to room temperature, unroll, cut into rounds, and bake.

Yield: 2 dozen

2 eggs

$^1\!/_2$ cup honey

2 cups unbleached spelt flour

$^1\!/_4$ teaspoon baking soda

$^1\!/_2$ teaspoon ground cinnamon

$^1\!/_4$ teaspoon ground allspice

$^1\!/_2$ teaspoon ground cloves

$^3\!/_4$ cup slivered almonds

$^1\!/_3$ cup finely chopped citron (optional)

1 teaspoon lemon extract

$^1\!/_3$ teaspoon unprocessed sea salt

◦◦ OATMEAL CHOCOLATE CHIP ◦◦
BANANA COOKIES

Yield: 2 to 2½ dozen

¾ cup whole evaporated cane juice

2 sticks (1 cup) organic butter, at room temperature

3 ripe bananas, mashed

2 eggs

1 teaspoon vanilla extract

2 cups spelt flour

1 teaspoon baking soda

¼ teaspoon baking powder

1 teaspoon ground cinnamon

1 teaspoon ground cloves

½ teaspoon unprocessed sea salt

2 cups rolled oats

1 cup chocolate chips, sweetened with grain or evaporated cane juice

This is a fun twist on one of our favorite cookies: the oatmeal chocolate chip cookie. Keep in mind, oats are a whole grain that is great to have in our diet, but more importantly, these taste great. The ripe banana adds a lot of sweetness to these favorites. This is a great snack that is a winner with everyone.

Preheat the oven to 375°F. Line a baking sheet with wax paper.

With an electric mixer, cream together the evaporated cane juice and butter until light and fluffy. Add the bananas, eggs, and vanilla and mix until well blended.

In a medium bowl, sift together the flour, baking soda, baking powder, cinnamon, cloves, and salt. Gradually add to the butter mixture, blending until well mixed. With a spatula, mix in the oats and chocolate chips.

Drop the dough by rounded spoonfuls onto the prepared baking sheet. Bake for 10 to 12 minutes, or until just starting to turn brown around the edges. Remove the cookies to a rack to cool.

～ PEPPERNUTS ～

This has always been a family favorite at

Christmas. These are small cookie balls with a light dusting of powdered sugar that have a slightly spicy bite. (See second photo insert.)

Preheat the oven to 375°F. Line a baking sheet with wax paper.

Sift the flour, cornstarch, baking powder, salt, black pepper, cardamom, cinnamon, and cloves together in a bowl.

In a mixing bowl, cream the butter and maple syrup together until light and fluffy.

Add the flour mixture to the butter mixture, alternating with the cream. Mix in the almonds.

Shape the dough into small balls, using mounded teaspoonfuls of dough. Place on an ungreased cookie sheet and bake for 15 to 18 minutes or until golden brown.

When slightly cool, roll the cookies in powdered sugar.

Yield: 6 dozen

2½ cups sifted spelt or unbleached white flour

⅓ cup cornstarch

1 tablespoon baking powder

½ teaspoon unprocessed sea salt

½ teaspoon black pepper

½ teaspoon ground cardamom

½ teaspoon ground cinnamon

½ teaspoon ground cloves

2 sticks (1 cup) organic butter, at room temperature

½ cup maple syrup

¼ cup cream

½ cup finely chopped blanched almonds

¼ cup organic powdered sugar

⤳ REAL GINGER COOKIES ⤳

Yield: 2 dozen

These soft ginger treats have a sweet and warming spice blend that makes the entire house smell like the holidays. They have a cake-like texture with small cracks on top. (See second photo insert.)

½ cup honey

½ cup unsulfured light molasses

1 stick (½ cup) organic butter, at room temperature

1 egg

1 teaspoon baking soda

¼ cup boiling water

½ teaspoon ground cinnamon

1 teaspoon ground ginger

½ teaspoon unprocessed sea salt

2½ cups unbleached spelt or wheat flour

1 teaspoon baking powder

2 tablespoons whole evaporated cane juice crystals (optional)

Preheat the oven 350°F. Grease a cookie sheet.

Combine the honey, molasses, and butter in large mixing bowl. Beat until the butter is creamy. Add the egg and stir until well mixed.

Stir the baking soda into the boiling water and, while bubbling, pour into the mixing bowl; mix well.

Add the cinnamon, ginger, and salt.

Sift the flour and baking powder together and stir into the mixture. Mix well.

Chill in the refrigerator for at least 4 hours.

Shape the chilled dough into a roll that is 1¼ inches in diameter. Cut into about ¼-inch slices and place on the prepared cookie sheet. Sprinkle the tops with the sugar, if desired.

Bake for 15 to 20 minutes or until small cracks appear. Because these cookies are dark, they do not turn golden brown like lighter cookies do, so you have to watch carefully for doneness.

∿⌒ **SNOWBALLS** ⌒∿

A simple and quick cookie to make, these are
a mix of crisp rice treat, baklava, and macaroon.
If you love sweet, crunch, and nuts, you will enjoy the
richness of this coconut-coated wholesome treat.

Combine the honey, butter, chopped dates, and egg in a saucepan and cook over low heat for 10 minutes. Stir in the cereal and chopped nuts. Shape into small balls and roll in the coconut to coat. Arrange on a baking sheet lined with wax paper to cool.

Yield:
6 to 8 servings

¼ cup honey or agave syrup

1 stick (½ cup) organic butter

½ cup dates, chopped into ¼-inch-thick pieces

1 egg

2 cups puffed rice cereal, preferably unsweetened

1 cup coarsely chopped almonds or walnuts

⅔ cup unsweetened dried shredded coconut

~◡APPLE CREAM CHEESE TORTE◡~

Yield:

10 to 12 servings

PASTRY DOUGH

⅓ cup expeller-
   pressed oil

1 tablespoon honey

¼ teaspoon vanilla
   extract

1 cup sifted spelt or
   gluten-free flour

FILLING

8 ounces cream
   cheese, at room
   temperature

3 tablespoons honey,
   divided

1 egg

½ teaspoon vanilla
   extract

4 cups unpeeled
   thinly sliced apples

1 teaspoon ground
   cinnamon

⅓ cup sliced almonds,
   lightly toasted

This is a delicious creamy apple pie with a toasted nut topping. If you'd like, rather than making your own dough, you can use a refrigerated piecrust.

Preheat the oven to 400°F.

For the pastry dough, combine the oil, honey, and vanilla in a small bowl. Add to the flour in a larger bowl and mix well. Add a small amount of water, if necessary, to create a soft piecrust dough consistency.

Press the dough into the bottom and up the side of 10-inch springform pan or torte pan with removable bottom. Set aside.

For the filling, combine the cream cheese, 2 tablespoons of the honey, the egg, and the vanilla in a large bowl. Spread over the piecrust.

Combine the apples, the remaining honey, and the cinnamon in a bowl and spoon over the cream cheese layer. Sprinkle with the almonds.

Bake for 10 minutes. Reduce the heat to 350°F and bake an additional 20 to 25 minutes.

❧ FRUIT KABOBS ❧

What a fun snack to create for a party!

Children might like creating their own. Since we just cut up a lot of fruit for the fruit pizza, here is another great fruit snack. It is colorful and a great afternoon snack or treat for guests.

Divide the fruit evenly among the skewers. Refrigerate until ready to serve.

Yield: 4 kabobs

8 strawberries, sliced in half

8 (1-inch) cubes cantaloupe

8 grapes

2 kiwi, cut into 4 chunks

8 (1-inch) cubes pineapple

4 kabob skewers (or for small children, straws)

‿◡ BAKED APPLES ◡‿

Yield: 4 servings

4 apples, cored

¼ cup coarsely
  chopped walnuts

2 teaspoons ground
  cinnamon

1 teaspoon ground
  nutmeg

2 tablespoons maple
  syrup

4 teaspoons butter,
  melted

This old-fashioned dessert is simple yet spectacular.

I love to eat them for breakfast, or you could top them
with Vanilla Ice Cream (page 109) or Natural Whipped
Cream (page 102) for a great dessert.

Preheat the oven to 375°F.

Score the apples to make a slit in the skin at the circumference.

Place the apples in four small individual ovenproof casseroles with
a tablespoon of water in the bottom. An 8-inch round or square baking dish can be substituted, just be sure to add ¼ cup of water before
adding the apples.

Combine the walnuts, cinnamon, nutmeg, maple syrup, and butter
in a bowl. Mix well and divide among the apples by spooning the mixture into the center of each apple.

Bake for 45 to 50 minutes, or until soft.

 BITE-LETTE APPLE CRISP

In the mood for a fast, homemade dessert?

This is quick and easy to make a single portion. The Bite-lettes bring the high quality sweeteners and oils, so all you need to do is sprinkle and bake.

Preheat the oven to 300°F.

Place the apple slices in an ovenproof container. Break up the Bite-lettes over the top of the apple.

Bake for 20 to 30 minutes, or until soft and slightly caramelized.

Serve warm or cold with Vanilla Ice Cream (page 109) or Natural Whipped Cream (page 102).

Yield: 1 serving

1 apple, cored and sliced, but not peeled

2 Laura's Wholesome Junk Food Lemon-Vanilla Bite-lettes

✺ BLUEBERRY PIE ✺
PERFECTION

Yield: 1 (9-inch) pie

1 recipe OrganicButter
Piecrust or Organic Oil
Piecrust (page 99)

6 cups blueberries
(fresh or frozen)

½ cup agave or
maple syrup

3 tablespoons
cornstarch

1 tablespoon lemon
juice

1 teaspoon lemon zest

1 tablespoon organic
butter

½ teaspoon ground
cinnamon

½ teaspoon
unprocessed sea salt

There is something so striking about blueberry pie. The rich, dark blue color and the taste of the berries in my mouth are so good. This pie has the great taste of blueberries sweetened with agave or maple syrup with the hint of citrus from the lemon. It is perfection.

Preheat the oven to 425°F. Line a 9-inch pie pan with one of the piecrusts.

Combine the blueberries, agave syrup, cornstarch, lemon juice, lemon zest, butter, cinnamon, and sea salt in a large bowl.

Pour the blueberry mixture into the piecrust.

Make several slits in the remaining piecrust to allow the steam to vent. Place the piecrust over the blueberry filling and crimp the edge.

Bake for 10 minutes, and then reduce the temperature to 300°F and bake for another 20 to 30 minutes, checking every 10 minutes, until the blueberry filling is bubbling out and the crust is golden brown at the edge.

Lemon Pound Cake (page 58)
with Raspberry Sauce (page 112)

Golden Pineapple-Carrot Muffins (page 67)

Rainbow Trail Mix (page 39), Honey Toasted Granola (page 28), and Fruit-and-Nut Trail Mix (page 37)

Boston Creme Pie (page 52) with Custard Filling
(page 70) and Chocolate Ganache (page 68)

Top to Bottom: **Potato Candy (page 48)**,
Haystacks (page 43), and **Maple Sugar (page 46)**

Apple Pie with Spelt Crust (page 91)

Mini Pumpkin Pies (page 94)

Grilled Cheese Squares (page 159)

Yogurt with Honey Toasted Granola
(page 28) and Raspberry Sauce (page 112)

⌁ CHERRY PIE ⌁

Typically cherry pies are mostly filled with goopy red cherry stuff and a few cherries here and there. Not this pie. This is an old-fashioned cherry pie that I love. We used to pick the cherries from a neighbor's tree when they offered or we would buy cans of sour cherries. This has lots of real cherries with the tart and sweet together.

Preheat the oven to 425°F. Line one of the piecrusts in a 9-inch pie pan.

Combine the cherries and almond extract in a large bowl.

In a small bowl combine the sugar, flour, tapioca, and salt. Pour the dry ingredients over the cherries and stir well. Let the mixture sit for 10 minutes for the tapioca to absorb the liquid.

Pour the filling into the piecrust. Dot with the butter.

Cut slits in the remaining piecrust and place over the cherry filling. Crimp the edge.

Bake for 10 minutes, and then reduce the temperature to 300°F and bake for another 20 to 30 minutes.

Yield:
8 to 10 servings

1 recipe Organic Butter Piecrust or Organic Oil Piecrust (page 99)

5 cups fresh sour cherries, pitted, or canned, undrained

1/2 teaspoon almond extract

1/2 cup evaporated cane sugar

4 tablespoons flour or 3 tablespoons cornstarch

2 teaspoons quick tapioca

1/8 teaspoon unprocessed sea salt

1 tablespoon organic butter, at room temperature

~ CRANBERRY PECAN PIE ~

Yield: 1 (9-inch) pie

1 recipe single-crust piecrust (pages 100–101)

1 cup chopped cranberries

1 cup pecan halves

3 eggs

2/3 cup maple syrup

1/3 cup cooked mashed pumpkin, or canned pumpkin

1/4 teaspoon unprocessed salt

We all know how good cranberries are for us.

With nuts, maple syrup, and fresh cranberries, this sweet and sour pie hits the spot. Serve it plain or with vanilla ice cream. This recipe is best made with either the press-in or roll-out crust.

Preheat the oven to 425°F. Line a pie pan with the piecrust.

Sprinkle the cranberries in the pie shell. Arrange the pecans on top of the cranberries.

Beat the eggs in a bowl until just blended. Add the maple syrup, pumpkin, and salt and blend well.

Pour the egg mixture slowly over the cranberries and pecans.

Bake for 10 minutes, and then reduce the temperature to 300°F and bake for another 20 to 30 minutes.

~ FRESH BLUEBERRY PIE ~

This pie is different than the Blueberry Pie

Perfection (page 86) in that most of the blueberries are uncooked
and it does not have a top crust. The crust is cooked separately from
the filling and the pie is served chilled. The sweet fresh blueberries
plus the dark cooked berries accented with a hint of lemon is
the perfect blend for a light, wholesome dessert.

Preheat the oven to 350°F.

Bring 1 cup fresh or frozen blueberries, the cane juice, salt, and
3/4 cup of the water to a simmer in a saucepan over medium heat for 10
minutes.

Whisk the cornstarch and the remaining 1/4 cup water together in a
small bowl until the lumps are gone and add to the hot blueberries.

Let the mixture simmer slowly until thickened.

Add the butter and remove from the heat. Add the lemon juice and
lemon zest.

Mix in 3 cups fresh blueberries and allow the mixture to chill in the
refrigerator for 1 hour.

When chilled, pour the filling into the piecrust and allow the pie to
set for 1 hour in the refrigerator.

Serve with Natural Whipped Cream, if desired.

Yield:
6 to 8 servings

1 cup blueberries
(fresh or frozen)

2/3 cup evaporated
cane juice, agave
syrup, honey, or
maple syrup

1/4 teaspoon sea salt

1 cup water, divided

3 tablespoons
cornstarch

1 tablespoon organic
butter or expeller-
pressed oil

2 teaspoons lemon
juice

1/4 teaspoon lemon zest

3 cups fresh blueberries

1 recipe any single-crust
piecrust, baked
(pages 100-101)

Natural Whipped
Cream (page 102)
(optional)

⌢ FRESH FRUIT PIZZA PIE ⌢

Yield: 8 servings

CRUST

⅓ cup expeller-pressed or organic canola or grapeseed oil

2 tablespoons agave syrup

1 egg

1⅓ cups spelt flour, white spelt flour, or gluten-free flour

1 teaspoon cream of tartar

½ teaspoon baking soda

½ teaspoon sea salt

FILLING

8 ounces all-natural or organic cream cheese, at room temperature

1 tablespoon agave syrup

1 banana, sliced

2 tablespoons lemon juice (optional)

1 cup sliced fresh strawberries

2 kiwi, peeled and sliced

1 cup blueberries

1 cup sliced fresh peaches

This looks like a pizza but is decorated like one of those elegant fresh fruit tarts in magazines. You can vary the fruit of this colorful, summery dessert. I love mixing strawberries, kiwi, blueberries, and peaches. Use fresh fruit only—no frozen or canned fruit.

Preheat the oven to 350°F.

For the crust, combine the oil, agave syrup, and egg in a large mixing bowl and beat well.

Sift the flour, cream of tartar, baking soda, and sea salt together and add to creamed mixture, mixing well.

Press into the bottom and up the side of a 12-inch round pizza pan. Bake for 12 to 15 minutes and let cool.

For the filling, whip the cream cheese and agave syrup with an electric mixer. Spread over the bottom of the baked crust.

Put the banana slices, if desired, in a small bowl and add the lemon juice, stirring gently.

Arrange the bananas, strawberries, kiwi, blueberries, and peaches in a decorative pattern over the cream cheese. Cut like pizza and serve.

 APPLE PIE

I like to leave the peel on the apples for color and nutrition. This pie is so yummy with the natural tartness of the apples, the slight sweetness from the agave syrup, and the gentle, warming spices. This is delicious with Natural Whipped Cream (page 102) or Vanilla Ice Cream (page 109).

Preheat the oven to 450°F. Line a 9-inch pie pan with one of the piecrusts.

In a large bowl, combine the apples, sugar, cinnamon, nutmeg, and salt. Mix well.

Pour the filling into the pie pan and dot with the butter.

Place the remaining piecrust over the apples. Crimp the edges and cut slits to allow the steam to vent.

Bake for 20 minutes. Reduce the heat to 325°F and bake for 30 minutes, or until the crust is light golden in color.

NOTE: For a shiny crust, brush the top with egg white, oil, or butter before baking. (See first photo insert.)

Yield:
8 to 10 servings

1 recipe Organic Butter Piecrust or Organic Oil Piecrust (page 99)

8 cups unpeeled thinly sliced apples

½ cup whole evaporated cane sugar

1 teaspoon ground cinnamon

1 teaspoon ground nutmeg

¼ teaspoon unprocessed sea salt

1 tablespoon organic butter, at room temperature

～◡ LEMON SQUARES ◡～

Yield: 16 squares

CRUST

1 cup spelt flour

2 tablespoons
powdered sugar

1 stick (1/2 cup) organic
butter or 1/3 cup
expeller-pressed oil

FILLING

2 eggs

1/4 cup agave syrup

1/3 cup evaporated
cane juice

3 tablespoons lemon
juice

2 teaspoons finely
grated lemon zest

2 tablespoons
cornstarch

1/2 teaspoon non-
aluminum baking
powder

1/4 teaspoon sea salt

The right lemon square has the perfect sweet and tart combination with a slight crust. Bite size and tangy, these are a great item to bring to a gathering as they can be served from the pan.

Preheat the oven to 350°F. Grease an 8-inch square baking dish.

For the crust, combine the flour and powdered sugar in a bowl. Cut in the butter until the texture is a coarse meal.

Pat the crust into the prepared pan to cover the bottom, allowing a slight lip of 1/2 inch around the edges to prevent the filling from spilling out.

Bake the crust for 10 minutes. Decrease the oven temperature to 300°F.

For the filling, put the eggs, agave syrup, evaporated cane juice, lemon juice, lemon zest, cornstarch, baking powder, and sea salt into a blender or food processor bowl and process until mixed well. Pour over the crust.

Place the pan back in the oven and bake for 15 to 20 minutes. The top should appear to have a fine crust.

Remove from the oven and cool for at least 30 minutes. Cut into 1- to 2-inch squares.

⌒◡ MILK CHOCOLATE ◡⌒
CREAM PIE

This rich and wholesome pie has just the right amount of chocolate plus some rich whipped cream with a hint of sweetness. Without being heavy, this is a perfect dinner dessert pie.

Combine the cocoa powder, milk, cornstarch, dates, salt, and eggs in a blender and blend until smooth. Pour into a heavy cooking pot and cook over medium heat, stirring constantly.

Reduce the heat to low and simmer for a few minutes, until thickened. (It takes a little longer if you use agave syrup.)

Remove from the heat and add the butter and vanilla. Cool for 30 minutes.

Whip the cream until stiff and fold into the chocolate.

Spoon the filling into the piecrust and chill for 1 hour.

Serve plain or with Natural Whipped Cream.

Yield:
  8 to 10 servings

½ cup cocoa powder

3¾ cups organic milk

4½ tablespoons
  cornstarch

⅔ cup chopped dates
  or agave syrup

¾ teaspoon sea salt

3 eggs

3 tablespoons organic
  butter

3 teaspoons vanilla
  extract

½ cup organic
  whipping cream

1 (9-inch) piecrust,
  baked (page 100–101)

Natural Whipped
  Cream (page 102)

Agave Syrup—Natural Sweetener
Agave syrup comes from a cactus and looks like honey but is not as sweet. It is good to use in baking, in drinks, or drizzled on something you would use honey on. It's vegan.

∿ MINI PUMPKIN PIES ∿

Yield: 10 to 20 mini-pies

1 (16-ounce) can plain pumpkin (not pie filling)

3 eggs

1 cup organic milk

¼ to ⅓ cup agave or maple syrup (or more to taste)

2 teaspoons ground cinnamon

1 teaspoon ground ginger

½ teaspoon ground nutmeg

½ teaspoon sea salt

With no refined sugar and all natural ingredients, this is a wholesome treat to enjoy all year long, and a great way to turn pumpkin pie into a lunch-box treat. If you want a crust, you can use a regular crust or buy a gluten-free mix and just bake like a regular pie, but I like to make them crustless. (See first photo insert.)

Preheat the oven to 300°F. Line 10 to 20 muffin cups with paper liners.

Place the pumpkin, eggs, milk, agave syrup, cinnamon, ginger, nutmeg, and salt into a blender or food processor. Cover and blend on high speed until smooth, about 2 minutes. Taste to adjust for sweetness.

Fill each muffin cup half full with the batter.

Bake for 10 to 15 minutes, or until you can touch the tops of the pies lightly with a spoon and no batter is on your spoon or until they crack a little on the tops.

A 9-inch pie will take longer to bake, Check for doneness after 20 minutes of baking.

VARIATION: To make a 9-inch pie, use our Organic Butter Piecrust or Organic Oil Piecrust (page 99) and halve the recipe, as a pumpkin pie uses only a bottom crust. Also as a substitute, you can use soy milk, rice milk or ½ cup coconut milk plus ½ cup water in place of the regular milk. (I prefer it with coconut milk.)

Herbs vs. Spices

Herbs are the leaves of the plant while spices are not. *Cinnamon* is the bark from a small evergreen tree that is native to Sri Lanka. *Ginger* is the root or underground stem of the ginger plant. *Nutmeg* is the seed/nut of the nutmeg tree, and the outer shell of the seed, when ground, becomes the spice mace.

∿ PECAN PIE ∿

This sweet and gooey pie has only maple syrup to sweeten it and uses pumpkin to create a rich, dark custard that coats the pecans. It is amazing how the pecans are placed on the bottom crust, yet, when baked, rise to the top to neatly to create this golden dessert.

Preheat the oven to 325°F

In a large bowl, beat the eggs just until blended.

Add the maple syrup, salt, pumpkin, and butter and blend well.

Spread the pecans over the piecrust. Pour the egg mixture slowly over the pecans.

Bake for 45 to 50 minutes or until set.

Serve the pie with a dollop of Natural Whipped Cream or Vanilla Ice Cream.

Yield:
8 to 10 servings

3 eggs

¾ cup maple syrup

½ teaspoon salt

½ cup cooked mashed pumpkin, or canned pumpkin

1 stick (½ cup) organic butter, melted

1 cup pecan halves

1 (9-inch) piecrust, baked (page 100–101)

1 cup Natural Whipped Cream (page 102) or Vanilla Ice Cream (page 109)

❧ RHUBARB PIE ❧

Yield:

8 to 10 servings

1 recipe Organic Butter Piecrust or Organic Oil Piecrust (page 99)

6 cups ½-inch pieces rhubarb

½ cup raisins

¾ cup whole evaporated cane sugar

⅓ cup flour (or 3 tablespoons cornstarch for gluten-free)

2 eggs

Natural Whipped Cream (page 102) or Vanilla Ice Cream (page 109)

Rhubarb has always grown in our backyard.
I remember picking it in the summer and tasting it raw. It was so sour! Yet, it has such a wonderful texture and taste when cooked in a pie. The combination of a sweetener and raisins is the perfect balance for the classic rhubarb pie.

Preheat the oven to 425°F. Line a pie pan with one of the piecrusts.

Combine the rhubarb and raisins in large bowl.

In a small bowl, combine the sugar and flour. Add the eggs and stir to blend.

Pour the mixture over the rhubarb and stir well.

Pour the filling into the prepared piecrust.

Place the remaining piecrust over the filling. Cut slits in the piecrust to allow the steam to vent and crimp the edge.

Bake for 10 minutes. Reduce the heat to 350°F and bake an additional 40 minutes.

Serve with the Natural Whipped Cream or Vanilla Ice Cream.

 RICE PIE

This dessert is like rice pudding in the shape of a pie. It has all the gooey comfort of warm pudding with a hint of cinnamon.

Soak the rice at room temperature in 2 cups of the milk in a bowl for 2 hours.

Pour the soaked rice and milk in a medium saucepan. Add the remaining milk to the saucepan and cook on low heat for 20 minutes. Set aside to cool.

Preheat the oven 350°F. Butter a 9-inch pie pan.

Cream the butter and agave syrup in a mixing bowl. Add the eggs to the creamed mixture and mix well. Stir in the rice and milk and the cinnamon.

Pour into the prepared baking dish and bake for 45 minutes.

Serve with the Natural Whipped Cream or Vanilla Ice Cream.

Yield:
6 to 8 servings

1 cup uncooked rice

4 cups organic milk, divided

2 tablespoons organic butter

¾ cup agave syrup

4 eggs, beaten

½ teaspoon ground cinnamon

Natural Whipped Cream (page 102) or Vanilla Ice Cream (page 109)

～◡ STRAWBERRY-RHUBARB PIE ◡～

This is a sweet and slightly tart pie that is a lovely pink color. It has a unique texture that is velvety smooth and rich. Perfect for a fresh yet traditional summer dessert.

Yield:
8 to 10 servings

1 recipe Organic Butter Piecrust or Organic Oil Piecrust (next page)

4 cups ½-inch pieces rhubarb

2 cups sliced strawberries (fresh or frozen)

⅔ cup warm agave or maple syrup

3 tablespoons cornstarch

Preheat the oven to 425°F. Line a pie pan with one of the piecrusts.

Combine the rhubarb and strawberries in a large bowl.

In a small bowl, combine the agave syrup and cornstarch.

Pour the dry ingredients over the rhubarb and strawberries and stir.

Pour the filling into the piecrust.

Place the remaining piecrust over the filling. Crimp the edge and cut slits to allow the steam to vent.

Bake for 10 minutes. Reduce the heat to 350°F and bake for an additional 40 minutes.

Top Crusts

Fruit pies often have a top crust, so that is when a two-crust pie recipe is needed. If you are making a pumpkin, pecan, or lemon meringue pie, you will only need a bottom crust. With a fruit pie, like blueberry, apple, or strawberry-rhubarb, you will use a top crust as well. The top crust serves two purposes: It helps seal in the heat to cook the pie, and it keeps the pie from drying out during the cooking process. However, the steam needs to vent, so a few slits need to be cut into the top crust. Or you can cut strips of dough and weave them into a lattice pattern over the pie. When a nice design is created with the top crust, the colorful fruit, like blueberry or cherry, will bubble over the pastry.

ORGANIC BUTTER PIECRUST

Using a fat that is hard at room temperature results in a slightly flakier crust. It is really a personal choice. When my mom was growing up, her mother saved chicken fat to use in piecrusts. If you love a flaky crust, then use butter.

In a bowl, combine the flour and salt. Cut in the butter until the mixture resembles coarse meal.

Add the water slowly until the dough gathers into a ball.

Roll out the dough between two sheets of wax paper to the desired thickness, laying the pie pan on top and allowing 1 inch extra for overhang.

Yield: 2 (9-inch) crusts

2 cups spelt flour
1 teaspoon salt
⅔ cup organic butter
¼ cup water

ORGANIC OIL PIECRUST

If you prefer a crust made from a vegetable oil, this one is good.

Combine the flour and salt in a bowl. Work the oil into it with a fork.

Add the water slowly until the dough gathers into a ball.

Roll out the dough between two sheets of wax paper to the desired thickness, laying the pie pan on top and allowing 1 inch extra for overhang.

Yield: 2 (9-inch) crusts

2 cups spelt flour
1 teaspoon salt
3 tablespoons cold water
½ cup expeller-pressed oil

～ PRESS-IN ～
GLUTEN-FREE PIECRUST

Yield: 2 (9-inch)
piecrust

2 cups Gluten-Free
Flour Mix (page 66)

1 teaspoon
unprocessed sea salt

¼ teaspoon baking
powder

¾ cup butter or
expeller-pressed oil

1 egg

1 tablespoon cider
vinegar

6 tablespoons water

If you don't want to roll out a piecrust,
here is a version that is easy to handle and can
be pushed in gently with your fingers.

Combine the flour mix, salt, and baking powder together in a bowl. Cut in the butter until the mixture resembles coarse meal.

Add the egg, vinegar, and water.

Press the dough into the bottom and up the side of a pie pan with your fingers.

～ LAURA'S WHOLESOME ～
JUNK FOOD PIECRUST

Yield: 1 (9-inch)
piecrust

1 to 2 (7-ounce) tubs
Laura's Wholesome
Junk Food Bite-lettes

Our wonderful cookies are soft and make a perfect
piecrust. Any flavor works, but I prefer the Extreme Fudge or
Better Brownie Gluten-Free for a wonderful chocolate crust
or the Lemon-Vanilla for a more basic and fresh crust.

Use about 15 cookies for a thin crust and 22 for a thicker crust. Press the Bite-lettes into the bottom and up the side of a pie pan to the desired thickness.

Pour in your desired filling and bake according to the pie recipe.

‿◡ ROLL-OUT ◡‿
GLUTEN-FREE PIECRUST

Some people prefer a crust that is rolled out.
This crust is tender and uses different grains than our press-in crust.

Sift the rice flour, tapioca flour, potato starch, cornstarch, baking powder, and salt together into a large bowl. Cut the butter into the dry ingredients, blending until the mixture resembles coarse meal.

Beat the egg and vinegar together and mix into the dough.

Form the dough into a ball and roll out between two sheets of wax paper, laying the pie pan on top and allowing 1½ inches extra for overhang. Peel one sheet of wax paper away from the dough.

Place the dough in the pie pan and remove the top sheet of wax paper. Trim any excess dough with kitchen shears and crimp the edge.

Yield: 1 (9-inch) piecrust

½ cup rice flour

⅓ cup tapioca flour

⅓ cup potato starch

1 tablespoon cornstarch

½ teaspoon baking powder

½ teaspoon salt

1 stick (½ cup) organic butter

1 egg

1 teaspoon cider vinegar

‿◡ GRAHAM CRACKER ◡‿
PIECRUST

Your basic graham cracker crust, which is
perfect for cheesecake and lemon or chocolate pie.

Stir the butter in a saucepan over low heat until melted.

Blend the graham cracker crumbs into the butter. Press the dough into the bottom and up the side of a pie pan and chill.

Yield: 1 (8 or 9-inch) piecrust

⅓ cup organic butter

1½ cups graham cracker crumbs

~ HOMEMADE ~
CHOCOLATE PUDDING

Yield: 6 (1/2-cup) servings

1/3 cup cocoa powder

2 1/2 cups organic milk

3 tablespoons cornstarch

1/4 cup maple syrup

1/2 teaspoon salt

2 eggs

2 tablespoons organic butter

2 teaspoons vanilla extract

Natural Whipped Cream (below)

This homemade pudding has a custard texture.

It is rich and chocolaty without being overly sweet. We serve it in parfait glasses for dessert or as an afternoon snack.

Put the cocoa powder, milk, cornstarch, maple syrup, salt, and eggs in a blender and blend until smooth.

Pour into a heavy cooking pot and cook over medium heat, stirring constantly.

Reduce the heat to low and simmer for a few minutes, or until thickened.

Remove from the heat and stir in the butter and vanilla. Set aside to cool for 30 minutes.

For an extra creamy texture, return the pudding to the blender and whip.

Pour into serving dishes. The pudding may be served warm or allowed to cool. Serve with the Natural Whipped Cream.

~ NATURAL WHIPPED CREAM ~

Yield: 1 cup

1 cup heavy whipping cream

1 teaspoon vanilla extract

1 tablespoon powdered cane sugar (optional)

Quick, simple, and versatile, this natural whipped

cream is an excellent topping for pies, puddings, cakes, and fruit. This works best using a chilled bowl and beaters.

Pour the cream into a mixing bowl and using an electric mixer beat until stiff peaks form. Add the vanilla and beat to blend. If desired, add the sugar and beat again.

VARIATION: For some spice, add 1/2 teaspoon cinnamon.

⤳ FRESH APPLE TOPPING ⤳

This is a favorite recipe that takes a few minutes and can be eaten plain or served warm over oven pancakes or potato pancakes (pages 166-167). Simple to make, the tartness of this topping can be varied by the type of apple that you use.

Put the apple slices, cinnamon, and water in a saucepan and bring to boil.

Reduce the heat to low and simmer for 5 to 6 minutes, or until tender.

Yield: 4 servings

2 apples, unpeeled, cored, and thinly sliced

¼ teaspoon ground cinnamon

2 tablespoons water

⤳ SUMMER ⤳
VANILLA CUSTARD

Custard is an old-fashioned dessert that has withstood the test of time. This treat has no trans fats and is so rich that you'll be satisfied with a small portion. The creamy taste of fresh custard combined with the colorful tart and sweet fruit create a sensual feast for both the eyes and mouth.

Beat the egg yolks in a mixing bowl until smooth.

Add the sugar and beat until creamy and light in color.

Heat the half-and-half or cream in the top of a double boiler until steaming hot.

Pour half of the hot cream slowly into the egg mixture, beating constantly. Add the egg mixture to the remaining hot cream and cook for 4 to 5 minutes, stirring until slightly thickened. Remove from the heat and add the vanilla.

Pour the mixture into custard cups or ramekins. Refrigerate for 6 to 8 hours until set.

Arrange the fruit on top of each custard and serve.

Yield: 6 servings

6 egg yolks

¼ cup evaporated cane sugar

3 cups half-and-half or light cream

1 teaspoon vanilla extract

½ cup sliced strawberries

1 kiwi, sliced

¼ cup blueberries

~ CHAPTER 6 ~
Ice Creams
and Toppings

When I was growing up, we had a hand-crank ice cream maker to which we had to add ice and rock salt in order to bring the temperature below freezing. I remember that we loved homemade ice cream; however, we did not make it often because it took so much effort.

Now, for a very reasonable price, there are automatic ice cream makers available. These have a container that you must freeze overnight that eliminates the need for ice and rock salt. Once the ingredients are in the bowl, simply turn the switch. Your ice cream will be ready in about 20 minutes. Clean up is just as fast and easy, and the container goes back in the freezer.

It is important to keep all of your ingredients cold. That means do not use a blender that has just come out of the dishwasher and is hot. The ice cream will never freeze. It is a good idea to put the blender in the refrigerator or freezer before using.

You know that the ice cream is done when it is thick like soft-serve. The ice cream you make yourself is initially softer than what you buy in the store. When placed in the freezer, it becomes harder than store-bought ice cream, because there are no added gums or additives to keep it soft. Also, the more sugar in your ice cream, the softer it will be. If you have homemade ice cream in your freezer, place it in the refrigerator about 1 hour before serving to soften it.

A small amount of unprocessed salt is added to bring out the flavors so that you do not need as much sweetener. We also use coconut milk in many of our recipes, which is good for people who are lactose intolerant. You can use organic half-and-half or cream if you prefer. You can also add any fresh fruit or nuts you enjoy to the ice cream.

Ice cream is a favorite dessert in many families. In my family, since we make it at home with quality ingredients, we have had ice cream for breakfast, lunch, or snacks. Our emphasis is on high-quality ingredients and great taste. These ice creams are so good, they are not just for dessert anymore.

ICE CREAMS

Chocolate Nut Chip Ice Cream

Lemon Drop Surprise

Orange-Pineapple Ice Cream

Peppermint Chocolate Chip Ice Cream

Piña Colada Ice Cream

Strawberry Ice Cream

Vanilla Ice Cream

• • • • • • • • • • • •

TOPPINGS

Blackberry Sauce

Blueberry Sauce

Chocolate Fudge Sauce

Raspberry Sauce

Strawberry Sauce

CHOCOLATE NUT CHIP ICE CREAM

Yield: about ½ quart

1 (13½-ounce) can coconut milk

1 frozen banana

¼ cup honey

½ teaspoon salt

½ cup coarsely chopped walnuts

¼ cup dark chocolate mini-chunks

With chunks of your preferred chocolate plus nuts, this ice cream is something you might have a small dish of as part of breakfast or a snack.

Place the coconut milk, banana, honey, and salt in a blender and mix until smooth. Pour into an ice cream maker and freeze partially. Add the walnuts and chocolate and continue freezing until done.

LEMON DROP SURPRISE

Yield: about 1 quart

1 quart half-and-half

½ cup honey

⅓ cup evaporated cane juice

3 tablespoons freshly squeezed lemon juice

1 tablespoon lemon zest

1 teaspoon vanilla extract

½ teaspoon sea salt

This ice cream is called surprise because I have never tasted a better lemon ice cream in my life. It is rich with just the right amount of sweet and sour. This recipe is from my friend Cole, who wanted to create the best tasting lemon ice cream ever. He tested this recipe many times before finding the right balance of lemon and sweetness.

Place the half-and-half, honey, cane juice, lemon juice, lemon zest, vanilla, and salt into an automatic ice cream maker and freeze. Run until the ice cream appears frozen and holds its shape.

VARIATION: To make dairy free, use two cans of natural coconut milk instead of the half-and-half.

ORANGE-PINEAPPLE ICE CREAM

Tangy and sweet, this refreshing ice cream tastes like a piña colada with an orange twist.

Yield: about 1/2 quart

Place the coconut milk, banana, honey, and salt in a blender and mix until smooth.

Pour into an ice cream freezer and add the pineapple and orange. Mix until the consistency of soft-serve ice cream.

NOTE: For best results, refrigerate all your ingredients the night before, or at least four hours before making the ice cream.

1 (13 1/2-ounce) can coconut milk

1/2 frozen banana

1/4 cup honey

1/2 teaspoon salt

1/2 cup coarsely chopped canned or fresh pineapple

1/2 cup peeled and coarsely chopped fresh orange (1 small)

PEPPERMINT CHOCOLATE CHIP ICE CREAM

A mouthful of minty goodness in every bite, this is a great holiday treat or a perfect after-dinner dessert.

Yield: about 1/2 quart

Place the coconut milk, banana, honey, peppermint, and salt in a blender and mix until smooth. Add the chocolate pieces and mix until combined.

Pour into an ice cream maker and freeze until done.

1 (13 1/2-ounce) can coconut milk

1 frozen banana

1/4 cup honey

1/2 teaspoon peppermint flavoring

1/2 teaspoon salt

1/4 cup dark chocolate pieces

~⌣ PIÑA COLADA ICE CREAM ⌣~

Yield: about ½ quart

1 (13½-ounce) can
  coconut milk

½ large or 1 small
  frozen banana

¼ cup honey or
  maple syrup

1 cup frozen fresh
  pineapple, chopped

½ teaspoon salt

The combination of pineapple and coconut has been
a longstanding winner. The banana is our main sweetener and
creates a texture as well. What makes this ice cream stand out is the
quality ingredient of fresh pineapple. You can really taste the difference
using fresh versus canned. This is wholesome enough for breakfast.

Mix the coconut milk, banana, honey, pineapple, and salt in the
blender until smooth.

Pour into an ice cream maker. Mix until the consistency of soft-
serve ice cream.

~⌣ STRAWBERRY ICE CREAM ⌣~

Yield: about ½ quart

1 (13½-ounce) can
  coconut milk

½ large or 1 small
  frozen banana

¼ cup honey or
  maple syrup

1 cup frozen unsweet-
  ened strawberries

½ teaspoon salt

This ice cream is pink and delicious.
The natural strawberry creates a beautiful looking and tasting ice
cream. What a perfect breakfast, after-school treat, or summer dessert.

Mix the coconut milk, banana, honey, strawberries, and salt in a
blender until smooth.

Place in an ice cream maker and mix until the consistency of soft-
serve ice cream.

～♥ VANILLA ICE CREAM ♥～

This soft ice cream is perfect for ice cream sandwiches made with two chocolate chip cookies. It is also delicious by itself, on top of pies, or served with cakes. (See second photo insert.)

Mix the coconut milk, banana, honey, vanilla, and salt in the blender until smooth.

Pour into an ice cream maker and mix until the consistency of soft-serve ice cream.

Yield: about ½ quart

1 (13½-ounce) can coconut milk

½ large or 1 small frozen banana

3 tablespoons honey or maple syrup

1 teaspoon vanilla extract

½ teaspoon salt

When Organic Is Best

While some people eat everything organic, it is not practical or economically possible for others. If you need to choose where to spend your extra money for a better quality product, start with free-range and hormone-free animal products such as, eggs, milk, cheese, or meats. Strawberries are also safer when organically grown—or at least pesticide free.

I ask the farmers at the market if their products are organic or pesticide free. I am happy to buy the pesticide-free fruits and vegetables even if they are not "certified organic."

∿ BLACKBERRY SAUCE ∿

This blackberry sauce is the perfect
topping for ice cream or pancakes.

Yield: ⅔ cup

1 cup blackberries
(fresh or frozen)

1 teaspoon water

1 tablespoon evaporated cane sugar

Place the blackberries, water, and sugar in a small saucepan. Stir over medium-high heat until the water simmers.

If using fresh blackberries, cover, turn off the heat, and simmer until the juices are release, 2 to 3 minutes.

If using frozen blackberries, cover, reduce the heat to low, and cook for 3 to 4 minutes.

∿ BLUEBERRY SAUCE ∿

When I think of fruit sauces, I mostly think of
the red fruit ones. A dark and sweet blueberry sauce on waffles, pancakes, or ice cream adds an unexpected color and taste.

Yield: ⅔ cup

1 tablespoon evaporated cane sugar

2 teaspoons cornstarch

Pinch of salt

2 tablespoons water

1 teaspoon lemon juice

1 cup blueberries
(fresh or frozen)

Combine the sugar, cornstarch, and salt in a small saucepan. Add the water and lemon juice, then the blueberries.

Heat over medium-high heat, stirring until the sauce begins to thicken.

If using fresh blueberries, cover, turn off the heat, and simmer until soft, 2 to 3 minutes.

If using frozen blueberries, cover, reduce the heat to low, and cook for 2 to 3 minutes.

⌒◡ CHOCOLATE FUDGE SAUCE ◡⌒

This sauce is my personal favorite. It answered my question of how can I eat chocolate sauce and make chocolate milk and hot chocolate with high-quality ingredients and a lower glycemic index. This sauce is excellent and you can make it as sweet or as chocolaty as you wish. I created this sauce after I used some store-bought chocolate syrup only to realize that it was mostly sugar and very little cocoa. Using the store-bought syrup to make the milk as chocolaty as I wanted it, I found that the milk ended up too sweet. If I had the sweetness just right, there was not enough chocolate. Here is the solution to that. (See second photo insert.)

Yield: 1¼ cups

1 cup agave or maple syrup

Pinch of sea salt

¼ to ½ cup unsweetened cocoa powder

1 teaspoon vanilla extract (optional)

1 to 2 tablespoons water or expeller-pressed oil to thin (optional)

Warm the agave syrup in a saucepan on the stove over low heat or in a double boiler.

Add the sea salt to the warm syrup. Add the cocoa powder a little at a time until you reach the desired balance of sweet and chocolate. Turn off the heat and add the vanilla, if desired. If the sauce is too thick, add some water or oil a little at a time until it reaches the desired consistency.

This sauce will keep in the refrigerator for at least 2 weeks. It will thicken when refrigerated. To serve, heat the sauce in a saucepan over low heat.

‿◡ RASPBERRY SAUCE ◡‿

Yield: 2/3 cup

1 cup raspberries (fresh or frozen)

1 teaspoon water

2 teaspoons evaporated cane sugar

This brilliantly ruby raspberry sauce is great on the Lemon Pound Cake (page 58). This is a fast and easy sauce that dresses up any dessert or treat. What I love about making it yourself is that you know exactly what you are eating—wholesome fruit.

Place the raspberries, water, and sugar in a small saucepan over medium-high heat, stirring until the water simmers.

If using fresh raspberries, cover, turn off the heat, and simmer until the juices are released, 2 to 3 minutes.

If using frozen blueberries, cover, reduce the heat to low, and cook for 2 to 3 minutes.

‿◡ STRAWBERRY SAUCE ◡‿

Yield: 3/4 cup

1 cup fresh strawberries

1 tablespoon maple syrup

Any of the recipes that call for Raspberry Sauce also go well with this strikingly red, sweet strawberry sauce. We used the strawberry sauce on the banana split (page 45). Dress up ice cream, cakes, and even breakfast pancakes.

Chop the strawberries over a small bowl, allowing them to release their juices into the bowl.

Add the maple syrup to the strawberries and juice and mix well.

Serve over ice cream or waffles.

~CHAPTER 7~
Freezer Pops

I grew up on homemade freezer pops. They were one of the first foods that I was able to make on my own from start to finish. While it is logical to think that freezer pops are consumed more in warm climates, they are actually eaten all year round in warm and cold areas. In fact, Ben & Jerry's, which started in Vermont, was told by the bank to sell crêpes in addition to ice cream because the bank did not think ice cream would be a success in a cold climate. Freezing almost anything makes it seem like a treat or makes it more fun. Then, getting to eat it on a stick makes it like play. Some of these pops will seem standard, yet they are made with high-quality ingredients. Others are more creative. I'd love you to email me some of your own creations: *drlaura @lwjf.net,* and tell me what you made and froze.

FREEZER POPS

Banana-Strawberry Pops

Cereal on a Stick

Chocolate-Banana Pops

Chuckling Chilly Chocolate Milk Pops

Creamy Orange Yogurt Pops

Grape Yogurt Pops

Hidden Candy Birthday Pops

Krazy Carrot Pops

Leaping Lizard Lemonade Pops

Merry Mellon Pops

Monkey Pops

North Pole Icicles

Peanut Butter and Jelly Belly Zebra Pops

Pink Banana Smoothie Pops

Strange Strawberry Milk Pops

Three-Melon Pops

Water Me Watermelon Pops

⌁ BANANA-STRAWBERRY POPS ⌁

You can combine any fruits or vegetables in these pops. You can stripe banana purée with grape juice or grape juice with carrot juice. Freeze each layer for 1 hour before adding the next layer. Your kids will enjoy seeing their artwork and colors in this creation. This is naturally dairy free, soy free, gluten free and nut free. (See second photo insert.)

Yield: 6 pops

1½ cups banana (fresh or frozen)

1 cup (8 ounces) water or milk of your choice, divided

½ to ¾ cup (4 to 6 ounces) strawberries (fresh or frozen)

Freezer pop holders

Freezer pop sticks

Place the bananas into the blender. Add half the water and blend. Add a little more water, if needed, until the mixture is milk shake consistency. Add the strawberries and the remaining water.

Fill the freezer pop holders to ¼ inch from the top. Press the freezer pop sticks in all the way, and place in the freezer for 4 to 5 hours.

When the pops are frozen, put the mold for the freezer pops in warm water for 30 to 60 seconds and pull gently to remove each pop from the mold.

～ CEREAL ON A STICK ～

Yield: 6 pops

2 cups yogurt or frozen fruit purée

½ to 1 cup granola

½ cup raisins

½ cup chopped straw-berries (optional)

¼ cup honey or maple syrup (optional)

½ teaspoon cinnamon (optional)

Freezer pop holders

Freezer pop sticks

Yogurt or fruit purée in a bowl with granola, raisins, and cinnamon and sweetened with maple syrup or honey is breakfast disguised as dessert. Choose your favorite Laura's granola (you can try other cereals but they may get soggy, while granola keeps its crunch) and you have whole grains and fresh fruit for a breakfast that feels like a treat. These pops can be made dairy, soy, or gluten free. For gluten free, you will need to use gluten-free granola, or just eliminate the granola altogether.

Combine the yogurt, granola, and raisins and strawberries, maple syrup, and cinnamon, if desired, in a bowl.

Add honey if you want it sweeter and cinnamon if you like some spice; stir thoroughly.

Fill the freezer pop holders to ¼ inch from the top. Press the freezer pop sticks in all the way, and place in the freezer for 4 to 5 hours.

When the pops are frozen, put the mold for the freezer pops in warm water for 30 to 60 seconds and pull gently to remove each pop from the mold.

These are creamy and soft and do not freeze as hard as the more watery pops do.

⚭ CHOCOLATE BANANA POPS ⚭

These could be called banana split pops

because it takes the best parts of a banana split: chocolate
and bananas. The bananas add a creamy texture.

Combine the bananas, milk, cocoa powder, and Chocolate Fudge
Sauce in a blender and process until smooth.

Fill the freezer pop holders to ¼ inch from the top. Press the freezer
pop sticks in all the way, and place in the freezer for 4 to 5 hours.

When the pops are frozen, put the mold for the freezer pops in
warm water for 30 to 60 seconds and pull gently to remove each pop
from the mold.

Yield: 6 pops

2 bananas

1 cup organic milk

1 teaspoon cocoa
powder

3 tablespoons
Chocolate Fudge
Sauce (page 111)

Freezer pop holders

Freezer pop sticks

～CHUCKLING CHILLY～ CHOCOLATE MILK POPS

Yield: 6 pops

1 to 1½ cups organic milk

Pinch of sea salt

¼ to ¾ cup Chocolate Fudge Sauce (page 111)

½ to ¾ cup chocolate chips or coconut (optional)

Freezer pop holders

Freezer pop sticks

These pops are a special treat in the most wholesome form possible. You might find yourself sneaking one for yourself while the kids are at school. These can be made dairy free, soy free, or gluten free.

Combine the milk, sea salt, and fudge sauce into a bowl and mix well. Begin with 1 cup milk and ¼ of the Fudge Sauce and add more of one or the other depending on how chocolaty you want them.

Fill the freezer pop holders, leaving about ¼ inch of space at the top. Drop in the chocolate chips or coconut, if desired, until the holders are full. They will fall to the bottom.

Press the freezer pop sticks in all the way, and place in the freezer for 4 to 5 hours.

When the pops are frozen, put the mold for the freezer pops in warm water for 30 to 60 seconds and pull gently to remove each pop from the mold.

Vanilla Ice Cream (page 109) with
Chocolate Fudge Sauce (page 111)

One Pan Eggless Chocolate Cake (page 59)
as Whoopie Pies with Fluffy Marshmallow Frosting (page 71)

Top to Bottom: **Real Ginger Cookies** (page 80), **Breakfast Macaroons** (page 75), and **Peppernuts** (page 79)

Ice Cream Sandwich with Chocolate Chip Oatmeal
Cookies (page 76), and Vanilla Ice Cream (page 109)

Banana Split with Vanilla, Chocolate and Strawberry Ice Creams (pages 108-109), Chocolate Fudge Sauce (page 111), and Natural Whipped Cream (page 102)

English Muffin Pizzas
(page 157)

Banana-Strawberry Pops (page 115),
Creamy Orange Yogurt Pops (page 119),
and Grape Yogurt Pops (page 120)

Chocolate-Banana Milkshake (page 139)

✦ CREAMY ORANGE ✦
YOGURT POPS

This is the first freezer pop I learned to make when I was about 3 or 4. It is still my favorite. You will love making this for breakfast. This pop is so versatile; plain yogurt, a variety of milks, or even a fruit purée will work for the base. The sweetness comes from the orange, which most kids like, and this creamy orange pop can be adapted to almost any food allergy. It can be made dairy, soy, and gluten free. Two ingredients and it tastes great. It doesn't get better than that! (See second photo insert.)

Yield: 6 pops

2½ cups (20 ounces) yogurt, milk, or fruit purée

¼ to ¾ cup orange juice concentrate

Freezer pop holders

Freezer pop sticks

Place the yogurt, milk, or fruit purée in a bowl. Add several spoonfuls of the orange juice concentrate and stir. Mix thoroughly and taste.

Add more orange juice concentrate until the mixture is sweet enough for you.

Fill the freezer pop holders to ¼ inch from the top. Press the freezer pop sticks in all the way, and place in the freezer for 4 to 5 hours.

When the pops are frozen, put the mold for the freezer pops in warm water for 30 to 60 seconds and pull gently to remove each pop from the mold.

These are creamy and soft and do not freeze as hard as the more watery pops do.

∿ GRAPE YOGURT POPS ∿

Yield: 6 pops

2½ cups (20 ounces) yogurt or milk, or fruit purée of your choice

¼ to ¾ cup grape juice concentrate

Freezer pop holders

Freezer pop sticks

This purple pop is fruit sweetened and pretty
to look at. Again, two simple ingredients yield tasty results.
(See second photo insert.)

Place the yogurt or milk in a bowl. Add several spoonfuls of the grape juice concentrate and stir. Mix thoroughly and taste.

Add more grape juice concentrate until the mixture is sweet enough for you.

Fill the freezer pop holders to ¼ inch from the top. Press the freezer pop sticks in all the way, and place in the freezer for 4 to 5 hours.

When the pops are frozen, put the mold for the freezer pops in warm water for 30 to 60 seconds and pull gently to remove each pop from the mold.

These are creamy and soft and do not freeze as hard as the more watery pops do.

HIDDEN CANDY BIRTHDAY POPS

This treat is perfect when your children want candy
and you want to give them something healthy. With this pop,
you can decide what kind of candy will be "hidden" in the treat.
Your child still knows that there is something special inside.
This can easily be made free of dairy, soy, nut, or gluten.

Yield: 6 pops

2½ cups (20 ounces) yogurt, milk, or fruit purée

Sweetener (honey or agave syrup), as needed

½ to ¾ cup candy (Gummy Bears, jelly beans, or chocolate chips)

Freezer pop holders

Freezer pop sticks

Combine the yogurt or milk and sweetener in a bowl. Taste and adjust the sweetness.

Drop the candy into the freezer pop holders.

Fill the freezer pop holders to ¼ inch from the top with the yogurt mixture. Press the freezer pop sticks in all the way, and place in the freezer for 4 to 5 hours.

When the pops are frozen, put the mold for the freezer pops in warm water for 30 to 60 seconds and pull gently to remove each pop from the mold.

⌒◡ KRAZY CARROT POPS ◡⌒

Yield: 6 pops

2½ to 3 cups carrot juice (only 2½ cups if adding peas)

½ to ¾ cup frozen peas (optional)

Freezer pop holders

Freezer pop sticks

This freezer pop combines carrot juice and frozen peas, two delicious vegetables found in one fun treat. This icy, yummy pop is simple to make and is naturally free of dairy, soy, gluten, and nuts.

Fill the freezer pop holders with the carrot juice to 1 inch from the top.

Drop enough frozen peas, if using, into the holders to fill them almost to the top.

Press the freezer pop sticks in all the way, and place in the freezer for 4 to 5 hours.

When the pops are frozen, put the mold for the freezer pops in warm water for 30 to 60 seconds and pull gently to remove each pop from the mold.

∿◡ LEAPING LIZARD ◡∿ LEMONADE POPS

Lemonade is so refreshing! Put it in the blender

with a few strawberries or raspberries and you have pink lemonade. Add enough lemon juice until you like the sour and then enough sweetener until you like the sweet.

Combine the water, salt, lemon juice, sweetener to taste, and the berries in a blender jar. Purée until smooth. If you are not using berries, combine all the ingredients in a bowl and mix well.

Fill the freezer pop holders to ¼ inch from the top. Press the freezer pop sticks in all the way, and place in the freezer for 4 to 5 hours.

When the pops are frozen, put the mold for the freezer pops in warm water for 30 to 60 seconds and pull gently to remove each pop from the mold.

Yield: 6 pops

2 cups water

Pinch of salt

¼ to ⅓ cup freshly squeezed lemon juice

¼ to ⅓ cup sweetener (honey or agave syrup), or to taste

A few fresh or frozen strawberries or raspberries (optional)

Freezer pop holders

Freezer pop sticks

⌇MERRY MELLON POPS⌇

Yield: 6 pops

2½ cups chopped ripe honeydew or cantaloupe

½ to 1 cup water, or as needed

Dash of lime juice (optional)

Freezer pop holders

Freezer pop sticks

Talk about an easy treat that takes a few seconds that just about any kid will eat! One ingredient combined with water in the blender and, poof, you are done. Fruit servings are taken care of for the week. By using melons of different colors, you are providing a variety of vitamins and nutrients for your kids. Make sure the melon you buy is ripe for maximum sweetness. This is naturally free of dairy, soy, gluten, and nuts.

Purée the melon in a blender. Add water and lime juice, if using, as needed until the mixture is the consistency of a thick milk shake.

Fill the freezer pop holders to ¼ inch from the top. Press the freezer pop sticks in all the way, and place in the freezer for 4 to 5 hours.

When the pops are frozen, put the mold for the freezer pops in warm water for 30 to 60 seconds and pull gently to remove each pop from the mold.

∽◡ MONKEY POPS ◡∾

This is like a banana split on a stick. You have your fruit serving, your milk or yogurt which is like the ice cream, plus "toppings" like granola, chocolate chips, or nuts. This can be made free of dairy, soy, and gluten. To make gluten-free, use gluten-free granola or eliminate the granola entirely. Make sure that the chocolate chips are also gluten-free and do not contain any barley malt.

Combine the bananas, yogurt or milk, and salt in a blender and purée. Pour into a mixing bowl. Stir in the granola, chocolate chips, or nuts.

Fill the freezer pop holders to $\frac{1}{4}$ inch from the top. Press the freezer pop sticks in all the way, and place in the freezer for 4 to 5 hours.

When the pops are frozen, put the mold for the freezer pops in warm water for 30 to 60 seconds and pull gently to remove each pop from the mold.

Yield: 6 pops

1 $\frac{1}{2}$ cups chopped banana (fresh or frozen)

1 cup milk or yogurt of your choice

Pinch of salt

$\frac{1}{2}$ to $\frac{3}{4}$ cup granola, chocolate chips, or nuts or a combination

Freezer pop holders

Freezer pop sticks

⌒◡ NORTH POLE ICICLES ◡⌒

You know how much your kids need water and how

much better water is for them than sweetened drinks. This recipe takes ice, which kids already like, and bumps it up a notch by hiding a small piece of fruit, like a grape, in the center. By licking their way to the hidden treat, they are getting pure, hydrating water. This is naturally dairy free, soy free, gluten free, and nut free.

Yield: 6 pops

2 to 2½ cups water

½ to ¾ cup bite-size treats*

Freezer pop holders

Freezer pop sticks

Fill the freezer pop holders with water, leaving about ¼ inch of space at the top.

Add the fruit or candy to the freezer pop holder and press the freezer pop sticks in all the way. Place in the freezer for 4 to 5 hours.

When the pops are frozen, put the mold for the freezer pops in warm water for 30 to 60 seconds and pull gently to remove each pop from the mold.

*NOTE: The treats can be any chopped fruit, such as grapes, apple, or orange (fresh or frozen), or candy (as long as it's healthy).

~ PEANUT BUTTER AND ~
JELLY BELLY ZEBRA POPS

Who doesn't like peanut butter and jelly? Here is a way to have them in a freezer pop. This can be made with any nut butter, so if your child cannot eat peanuts, you can use soy nut, almond or cashew butter instead of peanut butter. Nuts provide healthy fats, the fruit jam is sweetened naturally, and the yogurt is a source of calcium, protein, and energy.

Combine the milk or yogurt and salt in a bowl.

Add $^1/_4$ cup of the nut butter of your choice and stir. Taste and add more nut butter if needed.

Add $^1/_4$ cup of jam and stir. Taste and add more jam if needed.

Fill the freezer pop holders with the mixture, leaving about $^3/_4$ inch of space at the top.

Place 1 to 2 spoonfuls of the jam into each freezer pop until full. If using milk, the jam will sink to the bottom. If using yogurt, you may need to gently push the jam down with the spoon to the middle.

Press the freezer pop sticks in all the way, and place in the freezer for 4 to 5 hours.

When the pops are frozen, put the mold for the freezer pops in warm water for 30 to 60 seconds and pull gently to remove each pop from the mold.

These are creamy and soft and do not freeze as hard as the more watery pops do.

Yield: 4 to 6 pops

1½ cups yogurt or milk

Pinch of unprocessed sea salt

¼ to ¾ cup nut butter of your choice

¼ to ¾ cup fruit-sweetened jam or jelly

Freezer pop holders

Freezer pop sticks

～ PINK BANANA ～ SMOOTHIE POPS

Yield: 6 pops

1½ cups chopped banana (fresh or frozen)

½ to 1 cup water or milk of your choice

½ to ¾ cup strawberries (fresh or frozen)

Freezer pop holders

Freezer pop sticks

Smoothies are sweet and creamy mixtures that are often colorful as well. Here is my favorite smoothie combination that comes out pink. Knowing that the goal is three vegetable servings and two fruits a day, this fun pop can take care of the two fruit servings without giving your children unnecessary sweeteners. Feel free to change the fruit. Use water when possible instead of milk. This can be made free of dairy, soy, or gluten.

Combine the bananas and ½ cup of the water in a blender. Purée the mixture until it is the consistency of a thick milkshake.

Add the strawberries and blend.

Add more water if necessary to adjust the consistency.

Fill the freezer pop holders to ¼ inch from the top. Press the freezer pop sticks in all the way, and place in the freezer for 4 to 5 hours.

When the pops are frozen, put the mold for the freezer pops in warm water for 30 to 60 seconds and pull gently to remove each pop from the mold.

These are creamy and soft and do not freeze as hard as the more watery pops do.

⌒⌒ STRANGE STRAWBERRY ⌒⌒
MILK POPS

This recipe shows you and your child how to
create a pink drink by using only natural ingredients.
You can use the blender to make a pretty pink color that
provides a fruit serving with natural sweetener.

Combine the milk and salt in a bowl. Add $\frac{1}{2}$ cup of the jam and mix well. Taste, adding more jam for a sweeter pop.

If using strawberries, place the mixture in a blender, add the strawberries, and purée until mixed.

Fill the freezer pop holders to $\frac{1}{4}$ inch from the top. Press the freezer pop sticks in all the way, and place in the freezer for 4 to 5 hours.

When the pops are frozen, put the mold for the freezer pops in warm water for 30 to 60 seconds and pull gently to remove each pop from the mold.

Yield: 6 pops

$1\frac{1}{2}$ cups milk of your choice

Pinch of sea salt

$\frac{1}{2}$ to $\frac{3}{4}$ cup fruit-sweetened strawberry jam or jelly

$\frac{1}{2}$ to $\frac{3}{4}$ cup fresh or frozen strawberries (optional)

Freezer pop holders

Freezer pop sticks

∾THREE-MELON POPS∾

Yield: 6 pops

¾ cup chopped watermelon

¾ cup chopped honeydew

¾ cup chopped cantaloupe

Juice of 1 lime

1 tablespoon agave syrup, or to taste (optional)

Freezer pop holders

Freezer pop sticks

Made with three melons, this freezer pop is hydrating and refreshing on a warm summer day.

Combine the watermelon, honeydew, cantaloupe, lime juice, and agave syrup, if using, in a blender and process until smooth.

Taste and adjust the sweetness.

Fill the freezer pop holders to ¼ inch from the top. Press the freezer pop sticks in all the way, and place in the freezer for 4 to 5 hours.

When the pops are frozen, put the mold for the freezer pops in warm water for 30 to 60 seconds and pull gently to remove each pop from the mold.

∿ WATER ME ∿
WATERMELON POPS

You are about to make watermelon juice and

then a watermelon freezer pop. These are like eating a chilled slice of watermelon but better. This recipe, with only one ingredient, is so refreshing and tasty. Your kids will love removing the seeds from the watermelon and breaking up the fruit into chunks. This is naturally dairy free, soy free, gluten free, and nut free.

Yield: 6 pops

2 to 2½ cups chopped ripe watermelon, seeds removed

¼ cup water (optional)

Dash of lime juice (optional)

Freezer pop holders

Freezer pop sticks

Purée the watermelon in a blender. Add water, if needed, until the mixture blends into the consistency of a thick milkshake. Add the lime juice if desired.

Fill the freezer pop holders to ¼ inch from the top. Press the freezer pop sticks in all the way, and place in the freezer for 4 to 5 hours.

When the pops are frozen, put the mold for the freezer pops in warm water for 30 to 60 seconds and pull gently to remove each pop from the mold.

CHAPTER 8

Juices, Smoothies and Shakes, Milks, Hot Drinks, and Waters

We know that for thirst, water is the very best for our bodies. Hydrating our bodies is so important to our general health and energy level. In this chapter we talk about all kind of drinks, from spa water to drinks that can replace breakfast. We even have some treat drinks. All the recipes in this section call for organic milk of your choice and are sweetened with a wholesome sweetener such as honey or maple syrup. To make any of these recipes vegan, you can use water or plant-based milks and maple syrup or agave to sweeten the drinks that call for a sweetener. We use fruit for color, taste, texture, and sources of protein and fat. You can add an all-natural protein powder to any of the smoothie recipes for added protein and substance. (See sidebar on page 140.) For gluten-free recipes be sure to choose a gluten-free milk and protein powder. Most of the drinks in this chapter can be frozen into freezer pops if you prefer.

JUICES

Lemonade
Natural Pomegranate Spritzer
Natural Red Punch
Watermelon Juice

SMOOTHIES and SHAKES

Banana-Strawberry Smoothie
Chocolate-Banana Milkshake
Fruit Salad Smoothie
Mixed Berry Smoothie
Peach-Raspberry Smoothie
Tropical Smoothie
Yogurt Orange Smoothie

MILKS

Blackberry Milk
Blueberry Milk
Chocolate Milk
Mixed Berry Milk
Peaches and Cream Milk
Raspberry Milk
Strawberry Milk
Vanilla Milk

HOT DRINKS

Hot Caffeine-Free and Dairy-Free Chai

Hot Spiced Apple Cider

Natural Hot Mint Tea

Santa's Hot Chocolate

. . . .

WATERS

Citrus Essence Spa Water

Cucumber Essence Spa Water

Decorative Natural Ice

∿ LEMONADE ∿

Simple, easy, and refreshing. Keep a pitcher in your refrigerator when it is hot outside. I prefer to sweeten this drink with honey or whole evaporated cane sugar. The honey dissolves best in warm water on the stove. The whole sugar can create a light brown hue, but don't worry, that is the molasses component. Agave and maple syrup just don't seem to work as well here.

Yield: 4 servings

4 cups lukewarm water

4 teaspoons freshly squeezed lemon juice

3 tablespoons honey or whole evaporated cane sugar

Lemon or lime slices, for garnish

Combine the water, lemon juice, and honey together in a pitcher. Stir to dissolve the honey. Add more lemon or sweetener to taste and place in the refrigerator.

Stir just before serving. Garnish with a slice of lemon or lime.

NOTE: For a tasty limeade, use lime juice instead of lemon juice

~ NATURAL ~
POMEGRANATE SPRITZER

Yield: 4 to 5 servings

4 cups soda water

1 cup unsweetened
fresh or bottled
pomegranate juice

Lime wedges, for
garnish

Red punch says party. In this recipe we use
the natural goodness of pomegranate to add color and nutrition.

Combine the soda water and pomegranate juice in a pitcher. Pour into
wine glasses with Decorative Natural Ice (page 151).

Garnish with lime wedges.

~ NATURAL RED PUNCH ~

Yield: 4 servings

1 (12-ounce) can frozen
red fruit juice, sweet-
ened with fruit only

½ cup frozen apple
juice concentrate
(100% juice)

3 cups soda water

Here is a sweet punch that hits the spot
and is sweetened with only fruit.

Prepare the juice in a pitcher according to package directions, adding
an additional 1 cup water.

Stir in the apple juice concentrate and soda water.

Serve chilled.

∼◡ WATERMELON JUICE ◡∽

This is one of the most refreshing summer drinks.
It looks elegant in a wine glass or water goblet. It is terrific to
accompany breakfast or as an after-school drink.

Place the watermelon in a blender and process.

Add the water and lime juice to achieve the desired consistency.

Once blended, if the drink is not thick enough or cold enough, add ice cubes.

Yield: 2 servings

2 cups chunked fresh watermelon

¼ cup water (optional)

1 teaspoon fresh lime juice (optional)

3 ice cubes (optional)

∽ BANANA-STRAWBERRY ∾ SMOOTHIE

Yield: 2 servings

2 ripe bananas, broken
into chunks

²/₃ cup fresh stemmed
strawberries, or frozen

¹/₂ to ³/₄ cup water or
organic milk

1 teaspoon lime juice
(optional)

¹/₂ cup walnuts or
cashews (optional)

3 ice cubes (optional)

This is an excellent breakfast smoothie.

The banana adds a sweet and creamy texture to the drink,
while the strawberries provide a pink color and sour accent.
The banana is also a good source of potassium.

Combine the bananas, strawberries, and ¹/₂ cup water in a blender and
process until smooth.

Add more water, if needed, and the lime juice, if desired.

Blend in the walnuts, if desired, for some added protein and fat.

If the smoothie is not thick enough for you, add some ice cubes and
blend.

Frozen Fruit

A great way to save money and make a great shake is to use
frozen fruit. You save money by not throwing out ripe fruit but
by freezing it instead to use in a shake later, and using the
frozen fruit as the ice cubes makes a thicker, creamier shake
without needing ice.

CHOCOLATE-BANANA MILKSHAKE

What a way to put nutrition and dessert together!

A milk shake with natural sweeteners, fruit, protein, and minerals that tastes like a treat. (See second photo insert.)

Break the frozen banana into chunks.

Add to the blender with the milk and Fudge Sauce and blend until smooth.

Yield: 2 servings

1 frozen banana

1 cup organic milk or water

2 tablespoons Chocolate Fudge Sauce (page 111)

FRUIT SALAD SMOOTHIE

This is a great way to use up leftover fruit salad.

Any combination of fruit will work.

Combine the fruit, milk, lime juice, agave syrup, and ice in a blender and process until smooth.

Taste and adjust sweetness.

Yield: 2 servings

2 cups chopped fresh fruit

½ cup organic milk or water

Juice of 1 lime

1 teaspoon agave syrup, or to taste

3 or 4 ice cubes

～◡ MIXED BERRY SMOOTHIE ◡～

Yield: 2 (8-ounce) servings

½ cup apple juice or cider

¾ cup water

½ banana (fresh or frozen)

4 medium strawberries

¼ cup blueberries

3 tablespoons protein powder (optional)

This creamy, purple smoothie contains all the antioxidants of blueberries and is sweetened solely with fruit. If you'd like, you can add protein for more staying power.

Combine the apple juice or cider and water in a blender.

Add the banana, strawberries, blueberries, and protein powder, if using, while the blender is running and blend until smooth.

Protein Powders

Protein powders can come from milk, eggs, rice, soy, beans, and hemp. You may add them to any drink you want; however, I find that they can be gritty, add a greenish or brown tinge, or taste funny in certain drinks. I almost never use as much as the package instructs because taste and pleasure are sacrificed for the extra protein. It doesn't work for me. So, the thicker and darker the drink, the less you will notice the protein powder. Save it for thick smoothies. Mostly I look to get my protein elsewhere and leave the drinks alone.

❧ PEACH-RASPBERRY ❧
SMOOTHIE

Pink and fruity, this smoothie is a light
and nutritious way to start the day.

Combine the orange juice and water in a blender.
Add the banana, raspberries, peach, and protein powder, if using, while the blender is running and blend until smooth.

Yield: 2 (8-ounce) servings

½ cup orange juice

¾ cup water

½ banana (fresh or frozen)

¼ cup raspberries

½ peach or nectarine

3 tablespoons protein powder (optional)

❧ TROPICAL SMOOTHIE ❧

Can't get away to the tropics? Pretend you can
with this vitamin-rich, bright yellow smoothie.

Combine the pineapple juice and water in a blender.
Add the banana, mango, and protein powder, if using, while the blender is running and blend until smooth.

Yield: 2 (8-ounce) servings

1 cup pineapple juice

½ cup water

½ banana (fresh or frozen)

¼ cup chopped fresh mango

3 tablespoons protein powder (optional)

～YOGURT ORANGE SMOOTHIE ～

Yield: 2 (8-ounce)
servings

¾ cup orange juice

½ cup water

½ cup plain yogurt

1 teaspoon vanilla
extract

3 tablespoons protein
powder (optional)

For those who love creamy orange treats in the morning, this smoothie is great for breakfast.

Combine the orange juice, water, yogurt, and vanilla in a blender. Add the protein powder, if using, while the blender is running and blend until smooth.

Cutting the Milk

When making milks or smoothies, you always have the option to cut the milk with water. For example, when I make chocolate milk, I use ¾ cup milk with ¼ cup water or ⅔ cup milk with ⅓ cup water. I like it watered down to conserve on cost, but I also do not need my chocolate milk to taste that rich.

~⌣ BLACKBERRY MILK ⌣~

Blackberries have a great taste and color

that makes dark purple milk. They also have pronounced seeds that end up in the bottom of your glass. The addition of salt brings out the flavors a little bit, but be careful to add just a few crystals.

Combine the milk and agave syrup in a blender and process. Add the blackberries and salt, if using, and blend until smooth. Taste and adjust the sweetness.

Yield: 1 serving

1 cup organic milk

1 to 2 teaspoons agave syrup, maple syrup, or honey

2 tablespoons blackberries (fresh or frozen)

Pinch of unprocessed sea salt, just a few granules (optional)

~⌣ BLUEBERRY MILK ⌣~

Blueberries make a beautiful bluish-purple milk.

You don't need many blueberries, as their color is strong yet their taste is very mild. The lemon and salt bring out the flavors a little bit, but be careful to add just a few crystals.

Combine the milk and agave syrup in a blender and process. Add the blueberries and salt, if using, and blend until smooth. Taste and adjust the sweetness.

Yield: 1 serving

1 cup organic milk

1 to 2 teaspoons agave syrup, maple syrup or honey

2 tablespoons blueberries (fresh or frozen)

1/2 teaspoon lemon juice (optional)

Pinch of unprocessed salt, just a few granules (optional)

⤳ CHOCOLATE MILK ⤴

Yield: 1 serving

1 cup organic milk

1 tablespoon Chocolate Fudge Sauce (page 111)

Here is a sweet and satisfying chocolate milk made with natural ingredients. By keeping the fudge sauce on hand in the refrigerator, you are ready to make the ideal sweet and chocolatey drink.

Combine the milk and Fudge Sauce in a blender and process until well mixed.

⤳ MIXED BERRY MILK ⤴

Yield: 1 serving

1 cup organic milk

1 to 2 teaspoons agave syrup, maple syrup, or honey

2 tablespoons mixed berries (fresh or frozen)

Pinch of unprocessed salt, just a few granules (optional)

It may be hard to find one type of berry or you may not be able to decide on just one. You can buy frozen bags of mixed berries that you can use for flavored milks. These bags often contain strawberries, blueberries, blackberries, and raspberries. The addition of salt brings out the flavor a little bit, but be careful to add just a few crystals.

Combine the milk and agave syrup in a blender and process until blended.

Add the berries and salt, if desired, and blend until smooth.

Taste and adjust the sweetness.

⌒◡ PEACHES AND CREAM MILK ◡⌒

Since peaches are milder in flavor, we use more of them in this milk. I prefer to use frozen peaches, but fresh will also work. The addition of salt brings out the flavor a little bit, but be careful to add just a few crystals.

Combine the milk and agave syrup in a blender and process until blended.

Add the peaches and salt, if desired, and blend until smooth.

Taste and adjust the sweetness.

Yield: 1 serving

1 cup organic milk

1 to 2 teaspoons agave syrup, maple syrup, or honey

1 to 2 tablespoons chopped peaches (fresh or frozen)

1 tiny pinch of unprocessed salt, a few granules (optional)

⌒◡ RASPBERRY MILK ◡⌒

Raspberries are more potent in flavor than strawberries or blueberries. They make a tasty pink milk that will be a little more sour than Strawberry Milk (page 146). The addition of salt brings out the flavor a little bit, but be careful to add just a few crystals.

Combine the milk and agave syrup in a blender and process until blended.

Add the raspberries and salt, if desired, and blend until smooth.

Taste and adjust the sweetness.

Yield: 1 serving

1 cup organic milk

1 to 2 teaspoons agave syrup, maple syrup, or honey

1 to 2 heaping tablespoons raspberries (fresh or frozen)

1 tiny pinch of unprocessed salt, a few granules (optional)

～◡ STRAWBERRY MILK ◡～

Yield: 1 serving

1 cup organic milk

1 to 2 teaspoons
  agave syrup, maple
  syrup, or honey

¼ to ⅓ cup
  strawberries
  (fresh or frozen)

1 tiny pinch of
  unprocessed salt, a
  few granules
  (optional)

As a child I was not allowed to drink strawberry milk because it wasn't natural; then, as an a adult, I realized that that was easily remedied. This makes a great breakfast or snack drink. I like to use unsweetened almond milk. The addition of salt brings out the flavor a little bit, but be careful to add just a few crystals.

Combine the milk and agave syrup in a blender and process until blend well.

Add strawberries and salt, if desired, and blend until smooth.

Taste and adjust the sweetness.

～◡ VANILLA MILK ◡～

Yield: 1 serving

1 cup organic milk

1 to 2 teaspoons
  maple syrup, agave
  syrup, or honey

½ teaspoon vanilla
  extract

We have all enjoyed chocolate milk.
Vanilla is also a delicious and soothing flavor.
This is yummy served warm or cold.

Combine the milk, maple syrup, and vanilla in a blender and process until well mixed.

~HOT CAFFEINE-FREE~ AND DAIRY-FREE CHAI

A creamy, spiced drink that could
replace a morning coffee habit with the same comfort factor but without the caffeine or dairy.

Combine the almond milk, cinnamon, cardamom, cloves, salt, and honey into a saucepan over medium heat until steaming, but do not boil.

Strain the spices and serve in coffee mugs with a cinnamon stick.

Yield: 2 (8-ounce) servings

1⅓ cups organic almond milk

¼ teaspoon ground cinnamon

⅛ teaspoon ground cardamom

Pinch of ground cloves

Pinch of sea salt

2 to 4 teaspoons honey

2 cinnamon sticks

~HOT SPICED APPLE CIDER~

This traditional holiday drink is warming on cold
days and it makes the house smell good. This drink is especially nice served in clear glass coffee mugs.

Combine the apple cider, allspice, cloves, and cinnamon into saucepan over medium heat until steaming but do not boil.

Strain the spices and serve in coffee mugs with a cinnamon stick.

Yield: 4 (8-ounce) servings

1 quart apple cider

1 tablespoon whole all-spice

1 teaspoon whole cloves

4 cinnamon sticks

∿ NATURAL HOT MINT TEA ∿

Yield: 4 servings

¼ cup fresh mint leaves, divided

4 cups boiling water

1 to 3 tablespoons agave syrup or honey

I had this tea for the first time in a little breakfast place in Katmandu, Nepal. It was so simple, and I realized that it was easy to make at home and enjoy hot or cold.

Place a few mint leaves in each mug.

Add the remaining mint to the boiling water and turn off the heat. Add the agave syrup and allow to steep for 5 minutes.

To serve hot, pour the tea into mugs, distributing the mint leaves equally. The water should be a pale mint color.

To serve cold, chill the tea. When ready to drink, pour over ice and serve with additional fresh mint.

You may use maple syrup to sweeten the tea, but the brown color will show.

⌒⌒ SANTA'S HOT CHOCOLATE ⌒⌒

We would make this every year at Christmas for "you know who." The secret ingredient was vanilla. Little did I know at the time that vanilla was often mixed with chocolate because it gives chocolate a little something extra special. Even though we made this only once a year, this special drink can be enjoyed year round.

Yield: 4 (8-ounce) *servings*

4 cups organic milk

¼ cup cocoa powder

¼ teaspoon natural salt

3 tablespoons agave syrup or evaporated cane juice crystals

1 teaspoon vanilla extract

Pour the milk into a saucepan. Add the cocoa powder, salt, and agave syrup.

Heat over medium, stirring constantly, until steaming, but do not boil.

Remove from the heat and add the vanilla.

For an extra flourish, blend in the blender until foamy before serving.

CITRUS ESSENCE SPA WATER

Yield: 6 servings

6 cups filtered water

½ cup peeled, sliced ⅛ to ¼-inch-thick citrus fruit

Spas often have cool water with sliced oranges and lemon in it. Citrus fruits are energizing and refreshing. Store this water in your refrigerator at home or work and feel like you are at a spa. Using lemons and oranges provides a nice color combination. You may leave the peel on if you want more tang; however, it can have a slight bitter taste. I prefer to make this drink without the peel.

Pour the water into a pitcher. Add the citrus slices to the water and store in the refrigerator.

Pour into glasses over ice and serve with a slice of citrus.

CUCUMBER ESSENCE SPA WATER

Yield: 6 servings

6 cups filtered water

½ cup sliced organic cucumber, ⅛ to ¼-inch thick discs

Spas often have cool water with sliced cucumbers floating in it. Cucumber is soothing, cooling, and cleansing. There are expensive essence waters out there, so why not make your own? Store this in your refrigerator at home or work and feel like you are at a spa.

Pour the water in a pitcher. Add the cucumber slices to the water and store in the refrigerator.

Pour into glasses over ice and serve with a slice of cucumber.

∿ DECORATIVE NATURAL ICE ∿

When you have a clear drink or a punch bowl,

it is fun to do something creative with the ice. Use an ice-cube tray for individual drinks or a Bundt pan to make large ice-cube molds for a punch bowl.

Yield varies

Filtered water

$1/2$ cup fresh fruit, such as cranberries, rasp-berries, or blueberries

$1/2$ cup fresh mint leaves

Fill your ice-cube containers or Bundt pan with water, leaving $1/2$ to $3/4$ inch of space.

Sprinkle the fruit and mint leaves throughout and freeze.

Place 1 to 2 decorative ice cubes in each cup, or place the large round ice from the Bundt pan into a punch bowl.

∽ CHAPTER 9 ∽
Savory
Treats

Even though my personal preference is for sweet snacks, I also have a few savory ones that are deliciously rich and satisfying. These, too, can be made wholesome by the source of grains and protein you choose. Try to use hormone-free or organic cheese, when possible. If you need to avoid dairy products, try some of the alternative cheeses that use rice, almonds, or soy. When we call for eggs, you may use fewer whole eggs or egg whites instead. The goal here is satisfying food made with great ingredients that do not make you feel deprived in any way. They are exactly what you were craving.

SAVORY TREATS

Baked Sweet Potato Fries
Butternut Squash Nuggets
Corn Pancakes
English Muffin or Pita Pizzas
Greek Spinach Squares
Grilled Cheese Squares
Guacamole
Herbed Cornbread
Leftover Pasta Frittata
Leftover Rice Pancakes
Lemon Kale Chips
Melted Cheese Crackers
Oven Pancake
Potato Pancakes
Sesame Crackers
Sesame Cucumbers
Spiced Sweet Potato Rounds
Squash Blossom Quesadillas
Sweet Potato Pancakes
The Best Barbeque Sauce
Wholesome Quesadilla
Zucchini Pancakes
Zucchini Parmesan Squares

‿◡ BAKED SWEET POTATO FRIES ◡‿

Yield:

4 to 6 servings

2 to 3 large (about 1 to 1¼ lbs) sweet potatoes or yams, cut into wedges or french-fry strips

2 tablespoons extra-virgin olive oil

½ teaspoon sea salt

Colorful baked sweet potato fries combine some of the best tastes and textures. Some people like to add chili powder or spices. My favorite way of enjoying these is to eat them just plain. These need nothing except a napkin to wipe your hands with afterwards, but if you must have a sauce, try The Best Barbeque Sauce on page 173. This is a perfect after-school snack or side dish for a meal.

Preheat the oven to 400°F.

Place the prepared sweet potatoes in a large bowl and add the oil and salt. Mix well with a spoon or clean hands to coat all of the fries.

Arrange the fries in a single layer on a baking sheet or in a glass baking dish.

Bake, stirring every 15 minutes with a spatula to get all sides crispy. Test the fries to make sure they are thoroughly cooked.

Cutting Veggies Thin

When cooking vegetables, the thinner you cut them the faster they cook. If you choose to cut big potato wedges, they will need longer to cook through to the center. If you are in a hurry, cut thinner pieces of sweet potato, like thin french fries, and they will be ready much faster. It depends on your personal preference and how much time you have. No one likes to bite into a potato that is not cooked through, so make sure you test the thicker ones to see if they are ready. You may end up removing the thinner fries first, as they will be done if you have a mixture of sizes.

⌒ BUTTERNUT SQUASH NUGGETS ⌒

My friend Erika invented these golden cubes, which are similar to thick home fries with a deep yellow-orange center. A great after school snack or appetizer, these nuggets are really satisfying. The olive oil and salt and pepper enable the outer part to get crispy while the inner part cooks and becomes steaming hot and soft. I like dipping them in barbeque sauce or catsup.

Preheat the oven to 450°F.

Put the squash cubes on a baking sheet. Drizzle with oil and sprinkle with salt and pepper. Toss with your hands until the squash is coated.

Roast for 30 to 40 minutes, or until the edges of the squash cubes are brown and crispy

Yield:

4 to 6 servings

1 butternut squash, peeled, seeded, and cut into 2-inch chunks

2 tablespoons extra-virgin olive oil

Salt and pepper to taste

～ CORN PANCAKES ～

Yield:

3 to 4 servings

2 eggs

¼ cup organic milk (can substitute nondairy milk)

½ cup multigrain baking mix (not sweetened)

Kernels from 5 ears fresh corn

1 bunch green onions, chopped

3 tablespoons chopped fresh parsley

A few drops hot sauce

Salt and pepper to taste

Butter or olive oil

Corn pancakes are one of the most popular snack treats that I enjoy at my friend Erika's house. I knew the first time I bit into one that she had used fresh corn. They are terrific plain and are perfect for holding a household over until dinner. I have a hard time stopping at one—and sometimes they end up being my dinner!

In a large bowl, mix together the eggs, milk, and baking mix until well combined.

Stir in the corn kernels, green onions, parsley, hot sauce, and salt and pepper. The batter will look as if it is mostly corn, not like a traditional pancake batter; that's the way it should be.

Heat 2 tablespoons of butter in a heavy skillet over medium-high heat.

Using a few tablespoons of batter for each pancake, cook the corn pancakes in the oil until they are golden brown on both sides. Drain on a rack set over a baking sheet.

Continue with the remaining batter, adding more butter to the pan as necessary.

The pancakes can be kept warm in a 250°F oven for up to 1 hour.

Serve hot or at room temperature.

⌁ ENGLISH MUFFIN ⌁ OR PITA PIZZAS

Growing up, I remember this as one of the first snacks my mom allowed me to make by myself using the oven. I loved making my own pizzas as a kid! (See second photo insert.)

Preheat the oven or toaster oven to 400°F

Place the English muffins on a baking sheet and toast for 1 to 2 minutes to brown slightly.

Spread the spaghetti sauce over the top. Add the cheese and green pepper and pepperoni, if using, and place in the oven until the cheese is golden brown, about 8 to 15 minutes.

Cut into pieces or keep whole and serve hot.

Yield: 4 servings

4 English muffins, split, or 2 pita bread rounds (plain or whole grain)

½ to ⅔ cup spaghetti sauce

½ to ⅔ cup shredded mozzarella (or other cheese you enjoy)

⅓ cup finely chopped green bell pepper (optional)

⅓ cup chopped pepperoni or pepperoni substitute (optional)

~⌣ GREEK SPINACH SQUARES ⌣~

Yield: 2 dozen

3 (10-ounce) boxes
frozen chopped
spinach, thawed and
squeezed dry

4 eggs

1 bunch green onions,
chopped

½ teaspoon dried dill
(or 1 teaspoon
chopped fresh)

½ teaspoon dried mint
(or 1 teaspoon
chopped fresh)

1 cup multigrain baking
mix (not sweetened)

¾ cup crumbled feta
cheese

1 teaspoon
unprocessed sea salt

¼ teaspoon pepper

Imagine a delicious spinach quiche, with mint and dill accents, cut into bite-size portions. I love warm and filling appetizers like this one because they satisfy with their rich flavors and textures.

Preheat the oven to 350°F. Coat a 13 x 9-inch baking dish with cooking spray.

In a large bowl, combine the spinach, eggs, green onions, dill, mint, baking mix, feta, salt, and pepper.

Pour into the prepared baking dish and bake for 45 minutes, or until the top is turning golden brown and the mixture is set.

Let cool in the dish.

When cool, cut into 2-inch squares and serve at room temperature.

∿GRILLED CHEESE∿ SQUARES

My mom taught me this secret for making grilled

cheese: using mayonnaise to create a crisp surface and impart an extra comforting taste. You may not believe that something this simple can make a difference. This is one of my favorite comfort foods, and whether you decide to make just one sandwich and eat it yourself, or make several for a snack, it is a delicious, gooey treat. (See first photo insert.)

Heat a skillet over medium heat.

Spread a light coat of mayonnaise on 1 side of each slice of bread.

Arrange 2 slices of the bread in the hot skillet, mayonnaise side down. Top each with 1 slice cheese and sprinkle with the chives, if using. Top with the remaining 2 bread slices, mayonnaise side up. Cook until both sides are golden brown.

Slice the sandwiches into 1 to $1\frac{1}{2}$ inch squares and serve hot.

Yield:

4 to 5 servings

2 tablespoons mayonnaise or extra-virgin olive oil

4 slices whole-grain bread

$\frac{1}{4}$ to $\frac{1}{2}$ pound organic cheese, sliced $\frac{1}{8}$ to $\frac{1}{4}$ inch thick (may substitute rice, almond, or soy cheese)

1 tablespoon finely chopped chives or green onion (optional)

∿ GUACAMOLE ∿

Serve as a dip with whole grain crackers,
corn chips (preferably with sea salt), or raw vegetables.
Also makes an excellent sandwich spread.

Yield: 2 to 2½ cups

4 ripe avocados, pitted
and peeled

1 large bunch cilantro,
coarsely chopped

Juice of 1 large lemon
or 2 small lemons

Salt to taste

Combine the avocados, cilantro, lemon juice, and salt in food processor and blend until very smooth.

Taste and adjust the salt.

VARIATION: Salsa version: Add ½ cup of salsa, homemade or from a jar that has been preferably made with sea salt, to the guacamole for additional flavor. Add salt after you add the salsa as the salsa has added salt.

～ HERBED CORNBREAD ～

This is a childhood favorite of mine. I love this comfort food. It is delicious warm from the oven as a snack or reheated with melted butter on top.

Preheat the oven to 400°F. Coat an 8-inch square baking dish with cooking spray.

Sift the flour, baking powder, and salt together into a large bowl. Stir in the corn meal and herbs.

In a separate bowl, beat the egg. Add the milk, oil, and honey. Add to the flour mixture and stir just until moist. Pour into the prepared baking dish.

Bake for 20 minutes, or until golden brown. Cut into squares and serve hot.

VARIATION: This recipe can also be baked in a cast-iron corn stick pan. Bake at 400°F for 15 minutes.

Yield:

6 to 8 servings

1 cup spelt or unbleached wheat flour

1 tablespoon baking powder

1 teaspoon salt

1 cup corn meal

1 tablespoon dried Italian seasoning

1 egg

1 cup organic milk

¼ cup extra-virgin olive or canola oil

2 tablespoons honey

∿ LEFTOVER PASTA FRITTATA ∿

Yield: 6 servings

1 to 1½ cups leftover cooked vegetables, chopped chicken, crumbled bacon

2 to 3 cups any kind of leftover pasta with tomato sauce

8 eggs, beaten

2 tablespoons extra-virgin olive oil, plus more for cooking

⅔ cup shredded mozzarella cheese

¼ cup grated Parmesan or Romano cheese

Salt and pepper to taste

This is like an Italian omelet that uses leftover pasta and anything else you may have in your refrigerator: crumbled bacon, diced cooked chicken, leftover cooked vegetables, capers, chopped anchovies, or a few sun-dried tomatoes. Use your imagination; the possibilities are endless. Serve at breakfast or as a snack.

Position the oven rack on the second highest shelf. The rack needs to be more than a couple of inches away from the heat so that the frittata will not burn on the top.

Preheat the broiler.

Combine the vegetables, pasta, eggs, olive oil, mozzarella cheese, Parmesan cheese, and salt and pepper in a large bowl. (There needs to be enough egg that you can see it because the egg will surround the pasta in the pan and make a sort of omelet around it. But you don't want there to be so much egg that it's more egg than filling. It's a balancing act, and if you don't get it exactly right, don't worry, because it will still taste great.)

Heat an ovenproof skillet over high heat. Swirl in some olive oil, and then pour in the pasta-egg mixture. As the eggs set, lift up the edges with a spatula so that more of the egg can run underneath.

When the bottom is set and browned, transfer the skillet to the broiler. Broil until the top is golden brown, about 3 minutes. Remove from the oven and let the frittata sit in the pan for about 10 minutes to cool. The residual heat will cook the egg all the way through, and letting it cool will allow it to set up a bit before taking it out.

Loosen the edges with a spatula and slide the frittata onto a serving plate. Cut into wedges or squares and serve hot, warm, or cold.

⌒⌄ LEFTOVER RICE PANCAKES ⌒⌄

Think potato pancake but with rice instead.

They are crispy, flavorful, and a great snack to have on the
counter when the kids get home from school and are hungry.

Beat the eggs in a large bowl.

Add the rice, soy sauce, sesame oil, green onions, and edamame.
Mix well so that all the rice is coated with the egg mixture.

Heat a skillet over medium-high heat. Add 1 tablespoon of oil and
swirl in the pan. Drop heaping tablespoonfuls of the rice-egg mixture
into the pan to make small pancakes. Cook until golden brown on
both sides. Drain on paper towels.

Serve warm or at room temperature.

VARIATIONS: For *Italian Rice Pancakes*, omit the soy sauce,
sesame oil, and edamame and add $^1/_2$ cup shredded mozzarella
cheese, $^1/_2$ cup grated Parmesan cheese, fresh or dried basil, and
$^1/_2$ cup chopped sun-dried tomatoes.

For *Greek Rice Pancakes*, omit the soy sauce, sesame oil, and
edamame, and add $^1/_2$ cup crumbled feta cheese, $^1/_2$ teaspoon lemon
zest, $^1/_4$ cup chopped olives, and fresh or dried dill.

Yield: about 18
small pancakes

3 eggs

2 cups leftover rice, any
kind

2 teaspoons soy sauce

1 teaspoon sesame oil

$^1/_2$ cup chopped green
onions

1 cup cooked and
shelled edamame

Butter or olive oil

～ LEMON KALE CHIPS ～

Yield: 4 servings

8 large kale leaves, washed and dried

1 teaspoon fresh lemon juice

1 tablespoon olive oil

1/8 teaspoon unprocessed sea salt

I admit I was hesitant the first time I bought a bag of these in the store. Kale chips? We all know how important dark leafy green vegetables are, but would I really like these? For what they were charging, I decided I'd better love them… and I did. Then, I realized these chips were easy and inexpensive to make. They are light and crispy and satisfy your salty, crispy, crunchy chip craving in a wholesome junk food way.

Preheat the oven to 300°F. Line 2 baking sheets with wax paper.

Cut the kale in half lengthwise. Remove and discard the center stems.

Place the kale leaves in a bowl. Add the lemon juice and oil and mix with your hands, coating the kale. Sprinkle with the salt.

Spread the leaves in a single layer on the prepared baking sheets and bake until crisp, 15 to 20 minutes. Transfer to a wire rack to cool.

~꒰MELTED CHEESE CRACKERS꒱~

Melted cheese, whether organic cow's milk cheese or soy or nut cheese, is fun to eat. Cheese and crackers is a standard snack, and we often forget to take a few extra minutes to melt the cheese which completely changes the eating experience. Natural cheeses use turmeric or other natural ingredients to make a cheese orange, so if you like orange cheese, buy one that is natural and you will know that the ingredients are safe.

Yield: 4 servings

12 to 18 whole grain crackers or Sesame Crackers (page 168)

½ pound cheese, sliced ⅛ to ¼ inch thick

9 olives (black or green), sliced in half (optional)

Preheat the toaster oven to top brown or broil. Line the toaster baking pan with aluminum foil to prevent the cheese from sticking to the pan.

Place the crackers on the tray and put 1 to 2 slices of cheese on each cracker. Place in the toaster and bake until the cheese begins to bubble and brown, 5 to 10 minutes.

Place the olive halves on top of each cracker and serve hot.

◁◡ OVEN PANCAKE ◡▷

Yield:

4 to 6 servings

3 eggs

½ cup unbleached
spelt or wheat flour

½ teaspoon un-
processed sea salt

½ cup organic milk

2 tablespoons organic
butter, melted or extra-
virgin olive oil

This is like a chewy popover that is reminiscent of a
Yorkshire pudding but served as a snack with some baked apples.

Preheat the oven to 450°F. Grease a 1-quart casserole dish.

Beat the eggs in a large bowl. Slowly add the flour, beating constantly. Stir in the salt, milk, and butter.

Pour the batter into the skillet and bake for 18 minutes.

Reduce the temperature to 350°F and bake for 10 more minutes. Slice into wedges and serve hot. Or serve with the Fresh Apple Topping (page 103).

∾ POTATO PANCAKES ∾

Made with my Gluten-Free Flour Mix, this is a traditional potato pancake, or latke, which is great for breakfast, lunch or a snack. I like these served with Fresh Apple Topping (page 103).

Beat the eggs in a blender.

Add half of the potatoes and process. Add the remaining potatoes and process until smooth.

Add the onion and blend until smooth.

Pour into a bowl and add the flour mix, salt, and baking powder.

Heat a griddle over medium heat and grease with butter or oil.

Using a $1/4$-cup measure, scoop the mixture onto the hot griddle and cook until golden on both sides, 2 to 3 minutes on each side.

Yield: 9 pancakes

2 eggs

2 cups unpeeled, cubed potatoes

$1/3$ cup chopped onion

1 cup Gluten-Free Flour Mix (page 66)

1 teaspoon unprocessed sea salt

1 teaspoon baking powder

Butter or olive oil

⧸⧹ SESAME CRACKERS ⧹⧸

Yield: 2 dozen

1½ cups spelt flour, sifted

2 tablespoons evaporated cane sugar

1 teaspoon baking powder

¼ teaspoon unprocessed sea salt

½ cup organic butter or ⅓ cup extra-virgin olive oil

1 egg, slightly beaten

½ cup raw sesame seeds

These are delicious served plain, with cheese sliced or melted, or with your favorite dips. These crisp crackers are hearty and nutty but slightly sweet. The butter gives them that rich taste and full texture.

Preheat the oven to 350°F. Coat a baking sheet with cooking spray.

Combine the sifted flour, sugar, baking powder, and sea salt in a bowl.

Cut in the butter until the mixture resembles coarse crumbs.

Add the egg and mix well with a wooden spoon or your hands. Add enough water to form a soft dough.

Shape the dough into 1-inch balls and roll in the sesame seeds.

Place on the prepared baking sheet and flatten into 2-inch diameter disks with a greased flat-bottom glass.

Bake for about 10 minutes, or until crisp.

~⌣ SESAME CUCUMBERS ⌣~

This crunchy sweet-and-sour snack
is a big crowd pleaser.

Place the sliced cucumbers in a bowl. Drizzle with the vinegar and honey, and sprinkle the sesame seeds over the top. Add sea salt if desired.

Cover and refrigerate for 1 hour. Serve as an appetizer or side dish.

Yield: 2 servings

3 to 4 small Persian cucumbers, sliced lengthwise into thin pickle-like pieces

½ cup rice wine vinegar

1 tablespoon honey

1 tablespoon sesame seeds

Sea salt to taste (optional)

⌁ SPICED SWEET ⌁ POTATO ROUNDS

Yield: 8 servings

2 tablespoons extra-virgin olive oil

2 teaspoons garlic salt

2 teaspoons chili powder

¼ cup lime juice

3 large or 4 small sweet potatoes or yams, peeled, cut into ½-inch-thick rounds

Sweet potatoes are making a much-deserved comeback. In the past, sweet potato pie was a favorite. Now, burger joints to high-end restaurants are offering their version of sweet potatoes. These taste almost like candy. Are you in a real sweet potato mood? Make these gourmet rounds along with Baked Sweet Potato Fries (page 154).

Preheat the oven to 450°F.

Combine the olive oil, garlic salt, chili powder, and lime juice in a large bowl. Add the sweet potato rounds and toss to evenly coat.

Arrange the rounds on a baking sheet in one layer.

Bake for about 40 minutes, or until tender and browned around the edges. The exact time will vary depending on how fresh your sweet potatoes are—older ones tend to be drier and thus may take less time to cook. Serve hot or at room temperature.

~SQUASH BLOSSOM~ QUESADILLAS

Squash blossoms are the bright yellow-orange flower of the squash plant. They add a fun twist to a tasty snack. These cheesy quesadillas are great after school snacks or even for dinner.

Heat a nonstick skillet over medium-high heat.

Put 1 of the tortillas in the skillet. Sprinkle the cheese on top. Arrange the squash blossoms over the cheese.

Top with the remaining tortilla and cook, turning once, until the tortilla is golden brown on the bottom, about 3 minutes.

Cut into wedges and serve. Guacamole (page 160) makes an excellent partner.

Yield: 2 servings

2 flour tortillas

⅓ cup shredded Monterey Jack cheese

6 to 8 squash blossoms, washed, stems removed

～⌒ SWEET POTATO PANCAKES ⌒～

Yield:

4 to 6 servings

2 sweet potatoes,
  grated

1 egg

¼ cup unbleached
  flour

1 teaspoon salt,
  or to taste

Olive oil

Here is a tasty and wholesome twist on the traditional potato pancake. These golden orange delectable treats are comfort food with the better nutrition of a complex carb. These are great served warm as a pre-dinner snack.

Mix the sweet potatoes, egg, flour, and salt in a medium bowl until well combined.

Heat 2 tablespoons oil in a heavy skillet over medium-high heat.

Drop the batter by scant ¼-cup portions into the pan and flatten with a spatula to form 4-inch pancakes.

Cook until well browned on each side, pressing down to flatten while the second side cooks.

Add 1 tablespoon oil to the pan and repeat with the remaining batter.

Transfer to a wire rack set over a baking sheet to drain.

The pancakes can be kept warm in a 250°F oven for up to 2 hours.

THE BEST BARBEQUE SAUCE

My mother made up this recipe, and this is the barbeque sauce we grew up using. It is great for dipping vegetables, fries, or barbequed meat, or as a tangy replacement for catsup.

Heat the oil in a saucepan over medium heat. Add onion and sauté until tender, about 5 minutes.

Stir in the catsup, honey, Worcestershire sauce, salt, pepper, and Tabasco sauce, if desired, and simmer for 5 to 10 minutes.

Yield: $1\frac{1}{2}$ cups

½ cup olive oil

½ cup finely chopped onion

1 cup fruit-sweetened catsup

1 tablespoon honey

3 tablespoons Worcestershire sauce

1 teaspoon unprocessed sea salt

⅛ teaspoon pepper

Dash of Tabasco sauce (optional)

∿WHOLESOME QUESADILLA∿

Yield: 2 servings

Olive oil

4 tortillas (rice, spelt, or whole grain)

⅔ cup shredded Monterey Jack cheese

¼ cup finely chopped green onions

½ cup all-natural salsa

This is such a quick and easy snack for one person or to set out for a group. I like the rice or spelt tortillas best; however, whole grain or Ezekiel tortillas are good as well.

Heat a small amount of oil in a skillet over medium heat.

Place 1 of the tortillas in the skillet. Sprinkle half the cheese and half the green onions over the tortilla. Top with another tortilla.

Cook until golden brown. Turn over and cook on the other side until golden brown.

Remove from the heat and keep warm.

Repeat with the remaining tortillas, cheese, and green onions.

To serve, cut the quesadillas in wedges and dip in the salsa.

ZUCCHINI PANCAKES

These delicious zucchini pancakes are filling and satisfying. They are great served as appetizers or even warmed up for breakfast.

Yield: 4 to 6 servings

4 cups shredded zucchini

3 eggs

1 bunch green onions, chopped

½ cup crumbled feta cheese

¾ cup whole-grain baking mix (not sweetened)

1 tablespoon dried herbs, such as basil, tarragon, or oregano

Salt and pepper to taste

Olive oil

Drain the zucchini in a colander for 30 minutes. Using your hands, squeeze as much liquid from the zucchini as possible.

Combine the zucchini, eggs, green onions, feta, baking mix, herbs and salt and pepper in a large bowl until well mixed.

Heat 1 tablespoon olive oil in a heavy skillet over medium-high heat. Spoon 2 tablespoons of the batter per pancake into the skillet. Cook the pancakes, turning once, until they are well browned on each side. Don't flip the pancakes too early or else they will be very mushy on the inside and may fall apart.

Drain on a rack set over a baking sheet.

Repeat with the remaining batter, adding more oil as needed.

The pancakes can be kept warm in a 250°F oven for up to 1 hour.

～ ZUCCHINI ～
PARMESAN SQUARES

Yield: 2 dozen

4 cups shredded
zucchini

3 eggs

1 bunch green onions,
chopped

½ teaspoon dried
oregano

1 cup multigrain baking
mix (unsweetened)

½ cup grated Parme-
san-style cheese,
such as Parmigiano
Reggiano, Grana, or
Padano

1 teaspoon
unprocessed sea salt

¼ teaspoon pepper

This zucchini casserole is nutritious and rich.
Cut into small squares and enjoy as an after school snack.

Drain the zucchini in a colander for 30 minutes. Using your hands, squeeze as much liquid from the zucchini as possible.

Preheat the oven to 350°F. Coat a 13 x 9-inch baking dish with cooking spray.

In a large bowl, combine the zucchini, eggs, green onions, oregano, baking mix, cheese, salt, and pepper.

Pour the mixture into the prepared baking dish and bake for about 45 minutes, or until the top is turning golden brown and the mixture is set. Let cool in the dish.

When cool, cut into 2-inch squares and serve at room temperature.

Index